FRENCH MADE EASY

4:00 AM → Wake up
DRINK WATER
WARM LEMON

P O M O D O R O | **T E C H N I Q U E**

4:00 - 5:00 → LISTENING PRACTISE

5:00 - 6:00 → SPEAKING PRACTISE
6 → [BULLET COFFEE]

6:00 - 7:00 → EDITO / HW / REVISE

7:00 - 8:00 → WRITE CONJ / VERBS / VOCAB
EXCEL TODDLER METHOD

8:00 AM → START INSTACART
↓ GET READY / FAST
9:00 AM BRUSH / FACE ROUTINE
WASH ROOM

WATCH BBARTERS WHEN NO ORDERS

8:00 - 1:00 → INSTACART

1:00 - 2:00 → MON - THOR = ~~WORKOUT~~ & PROTIEN
FRI - SAT - SUN = PREPARE COOKING

2:00 - 3:00 → BBARTERS / REVISE

3:00 PM → START INSTACART

3:00 - 4:00 PM → BBARTERS / REVISE

4:00 - 8:30 PM → DASH & INSTACART

8:30 - 9:00 → WORKOUT
9:30 PM → SHOWER
SLEEP

FRENCH MADE EASY

By

Ms. Rashmi Varma

B.A. (English Hons.)

M.A. (French from J.N.U.)

GOODWILL PUBLISHING HOUSE

B-3, RATTAN JYOTI, 18, RAJENDRA PLACE
NEW DELHI-110008 (INDIA)

Published by

Rajneesh Chowdhry
for
Goodwill Publishing House
B-3, Rattan Jyoti
18, Rajendra Place
New Delhi-110008
Tel : 25750801, 25755519, 25820556
Fax : 91-11-25763428
E-mail : goodwillpub@vsnl.net
Website : www.goodwillpublishinghouse.com

Typeset at

Radha Laserkraft
R-814, New Rajinder Nagar
New Delhi-110060 • Tel : 28742031

Printed at : Kumar Offset Printers, Delhi-110092

PREFACE

French is a romantic language, although that's not why it's called the language of love. In linguistic terms, "Romance" and "Romantic" have nothing to do with love. They come from the word the Roman and mean "from Latin". French is spoken by about 124 million people in the world. Therefore, it is one of the most widely spoken languages in the world.

French and English are the only languages to be spoken as native languages on 5 continents. French is a Latin language, which means that it has the same roots as Italian, Spanish, Romanian, Portuguese, or Catalan.

French is the official language of France, and its overseas territories as well as *Bénis, Burkina Faso*, Central African Republic, Congo (Democratic Republic of), Congo (Republic of), *Côte d'Ivoire*, Gabon, Guinea, Luxembourg, Mali, Monaco, Niger, Sénégal, Togo, the Canadian Province of *Québec* and the Swiss districts of Vaud, *Neuchâted, Genève* and *Jura*.

Language learning should be quick, fun, and easy! Many foreign language students have difficulty learning. Our goal is to speak French naturally with others.

This book is an attempt to meet this need. It provides you with the vocabulary with which you can create new sentences, sentence patterns, correct pronunciation and dialogues, which will help you communicate in certain situations.

So, let's start speaking French now.

RASHMI VARMA

CONTENTS

1

INTRODUCTION

There are 26 letters in French as in English, but they are pronounced differently.

A	*aa*
B	*bay*
C	*say*
D	*day*
E	*e*
F	*ef*
G	*j*
H	*aash*
I	*ee*
J	*g*
K	*kah*
L	*el*
M	*em*
N	*en*
O	*o*
P	*pay*
Q	*koo*

	R		*er*
	S		*es*
	T		*tay*
	U		*eu*
	V		*way*
	W		*doobl-way*
	X		*eeks*
	Y		*eegrek*
	Z		*tsed*
[b]	B		*bon, bas*
[d]	D		*douane, dur*
[f]	F		*neuf*
	PH		*phare*
[g]	G		*gants, gris*
[ʒ]	G		*gèle, mangeons*
	J		*jaune*
[k]	C		*sucre*
	CH		*psychologie*
	CK		*Franck*
	K		*ski*
	QU		*quinze*
[l]	L		*le*
[m]	M		*comment*
			Marie

[n]	N	*noir*
		sonner
[p]	P	*soupe*
[r]	R	*rouge*
[s]	S	*sucre*
	C	*cent*
	ç	*français*
	SC	*sciences*
	SS	*poisson*
	TI	*attention*
	X	*soixante*
[t]	T	*tarte*
	TH	*théâtre*
[v]	V	*violet*
	W	*wagon*
[Z]	S	*visage*
	Z	*zéro*
	X	*dixième*
[ʃ]	CH	*chat*
	SH	*shorts*
[η]	GN	*peigner*

3

VOWELS
VOYELLES

[i]	i	*si*
	y	*pyjama*
[e]	é	*été*
[ɛ]	ê	*être*
	è	*crème*
	ai	*mais*
[a]	a	*patte*
	â	*pâte*
[ɔ]	o	*or*
[o]	o	*zéro*
	au	*au*
[u]	ou	*ou*
[Y]	u	*tu*
[Ø]	eu	*bleu*
[œ]	heu	*heure*

SEMI-VOWELS

[w]	ou	*oui*
[μ]	u	*lui*
[j]	i	*pied*

4

NASAL VOWELS
VOYELLES NASALES

[ɛ̃]	*in*	*vin*
[ã]	*an*	*an*
[õ]	*on*	*on*
[œ̃]	*un*	*brun*

2
ACCENTS
ACCENTS

There are 4 French accents for vowels and one accent for a consonant.

The *Accent aigu* ′ (accute accent) can only be on an E.

Example : *étudiant* student

The *Accent grave* ` (grave accent) can be found on an A, E or U. On the A and U, it usually serves to distinguish between homonyms, e.g.

ou or

où where

The *Accent circonflexe* ^ can be on A, E, I, O or U. The circonflex usually indicates that an S is used to follow that vowel, e.g.

fôret forest

It also serves to distinguish between homonyms. For example,

du (contraction of de & le)

dû (past particle of the verb 'devoir')

The *Accent trema* ·· can be on an E or U. It is used when two vowels that are next to each other have to be pronounced separately. For example,

naïve

Saül

6

The *cédille* ˛ is found only on the letter C. It changes the hard sound [K] into a soft sound [S]. The cedélle is never placed in front of E or I because C always sounds like [S] in front of these vowels.

On capital letters, one may or may not put these accents.

French pronunciation is different from the English one. The pronunciation table given earlier is based on French dictionaries and other French books. But the table given below will help you pick up the pronunciation with the help of English words.

Letters	Pronounciation
a, à, â	like father
b	like bat
c	like cake if followed by e & i, like save
d	like Delhi
é	like fate
è, ê, ai	like pet
e, eu	like further
eu, oeu	like treasure
f, ff, ph	like fate
g	like get if followed by e & i, like giraffe
h	never pronounced

i, î	like feet
j	like treasure. Never like Jam
k	like kite
l, ll	like London
m, mm	like Magic
n, nn, mn	like night
o, ô, au, eau	like broke
o	like pot
p, pp	like Paris
qu	like kite
r, rr	like the Spanish J
s	like sit or zip Never pronounced at the end of a word
ss, ç	like sit
t, tt, th	like time
u, û, ù	like the German ü Somewhere between e & u
v	like van
w	like watch
x	pronounced as ks or gz. Never pronounced at the end of a word
y	like yes
z	like zoo
ou	like zoo

8

ch	like **sh**ave
gn	like Ken**ya**
ill	like i+y
oi	like **wa**ter

S between two vowels is pronounced as Z. To get the [S] sound between two vowels, we put SS. For example,

rose is pronounced as *roz*

grasse is pronounced as *gras*

G and C have different pronunciations, depending on the vowels following them. Before the soft vowels E and I, G is pronounced as l j l, like in giraffe and c is pronounced as l s l, as in save. But before the hard vowels A, O, and U, G is pronounced as l g l, like in goat and c is pronounced as l k l, as in cat.

If you want to pronounce G as l g l before the hard vowels A, O and U, add E after G.

Example : George, Geography

If you want to pronounce C as l s l before the hard vowels A, O and U, add a cedille to the C.

Example : Français (pronounced as *Fransè*)

Francais would be pronounced as *Frankè,* which is wrong.

The vowels followed by N or m are known as nasal vowels, i.e. vowels that are pronounced through the nose.

These sounds don't exist in English, though they do exist
in Hindi.

Letter	Pronounciation
an, en, am, em, aon	like tarnish
in, im	like sang
on, om	like corn
un, um	like sang

3

NUMBERS
NOMBRES

Cardinal Numbers
Nombres Cardinaux

0	Zero	*Zéro*
1	One	*Un*
2	Two	*Deux*
3	Three	*Trois*
4	Four	*Quatre*
5	Five	*Cinq*
6	Six	*Six*
7	Seven	*Sept*
8	Eight	*Huit*
9	Nine	*Neuf*
10	Ten	*Dix*
11	Eleven	*Onze*
12	Twelve	*Douze*
13	Thirteen	*Treize*
14	Fourteen	*Quatorze*
15	Fifteen	*Quinze*
16	Sixteen	*Seize*

17	Seventeen	*Dix-sept*
18	Eighteen	*Dix-huit*
19	Nineteen	*Dix-neuf*
20	Twenty	*Vingt*
21	Twenty-one	*Vingt et un*
22	Twenty-two	*Vingt-deux*
23	Twenty-three	*Vingt-trois*
24	Twenty-four	*Vingt-quatre*
25	Twenty-five	*Vingt-cinq*
26	Twenty-six	*Vingt-six*
27	Twenty-seven	*Vingt-sept*
28	Twenty-eight	*Vingt-huit*
29	Twenty-nine	*Vingt-neuf*
30	Thirty	*Trente*
31	Thirty-one	*Trente et un*
32	Thirty-two	*Trente-deux*
33	Thirty-three	*Trente-trois*
34	Thirty-four	*Trente-quatre*
35	Thirty-five	*Trente-cinq*
36	Thirty-six	*Trente-six*
37	Thirty-seven	*Trente-sept*
38	Thirty-eight	*Trente-huit*
39	Thirty-nine	*Trente-neuf*

40	Forty	Quarante
41	Forty-one	Quarante et un
42	Forty-two	Quarante-deux
43	Forty-three	Quarante-trois
44	Forty-four	Quarante-quatre
45	Forty-five	Quarante-cinq
46	Forty-six	Quarante-six
47	Forty-seven	Quarante-sept
48	Forty-eight	Quarante-huit
49	Forty-nine	Quarante-neuf
50	Fifty	Cinquante
51	Fifty-one	Cinquante et un
52	Fifty-two	Cinquante-deux
53	Fifty-three	Cinquante-trois
54	Fifty-four	Cinquante-quatre
55	Fifty-five	Cinquante-cinq
56	Fifty-six	Cinquante-six
57	Fifty-seven	Cinquante-sept
58	Fifty-eight	Cinquante-huit
59	Fifty-nine	Cinquante-neuf
60	Sixty	Soixante
61	Sixty-one	Soixante et un
62	Sixty-two	Soixante-deux

63 Sixty-three	Soixante-trois
64 Sixty-four	Soixante-quatre
65 Sixty-five	Soixante-cinq
66 Sixty-six	Soixante-six
67 Sixty-seven	Soixante-sept
68 Sixty-eight	Soixante-huit
69 Sixty-nine	Soixante-neuf
70 Seventy	Soixante-dix
71 Seventy-one	Soixante et onze
72 Seventy-two	Soixante-douze
73 Seventy-three	Soixante-treize
74 Seventy-four	Soixante-quatorze
75 Seventy-five	Soixante-quinze
76 Seventy-six	Soixante-seize
77 Seventy-seven	Soixante-dix-sept
78 Seventy-eight	Soixante-dix-huit
79 Seventy-nine	Soixante-dix-neuf
80 Eighty	Quatre-vingts
81 Eighty-one	Quatre-vingt-un
82 Eighty-two	Quatre-vingt-deux
83 Eighty-three	Quatre-vingt-trois
84 Eighty-four	Quatre-vingt-quatre
85 Eighty-five	Quatre-vingt-cinq

86	Eighty-six	*Quatre-vingt-six*
87	Eighty-seven	*Quatre-vingt-sept*
88	Eighty-eight	*Quatre-vingt-huit*
89	Eighty-nine	*Quatre-vingt-neuf*
90	Ninety	*Quatre-vingt-dix*
91	Ninety-one	*Quatre-vingt-onze*
92	Ninety-two	*Quatre-vingt-douze*
93	Ninety-three	*Quatre-vingt-treize*
94	Ninety-four	*Quatre-vingt-quatorze*
95	Ninety-five	*Quatre-vingt-quinze*
96	Ninety-six	*Quatre-vingt-seize*
97	Ninety-seven	*Quatre-vingt-dix-sept*
98	Ninety-eight	*Quatre-vingt-dix-huit*
99	Ninety-nine	*Quatre-vingt-dix-neuf*
100	Hundred	*Cent*
200	Two hudred	*Deux cents*
201	Two hundred one	*Deux cent un*
1000	One thousand	*Mille*
2000	Two thousand	*Deux mille*
1000,000	One million	*Un million*
2000,000	Two million	*Deux millions*
1000,000,000	One billion	*Un milliard*

Ordinal numbers
Les nombres ordinaux

1st	First	*Premier*
		Première
2nd	Second	*Deuxième*
3rd	Third	*Troisième*
4th	Fourth	*Quatrième*
5th	Fifth	*Cinquième*
6th	Sixth	*Sixième*
7th	Seventh	*Septième*
8th	Eighth	*Huitième*
9th	Ninth	*Neuvième*
10th	Tenth	*Dixième*

Fractions
Les Fractions

1/2	a half	*un demie(m)*
		une demie(f)
1/4	one-fourth	*un quart*
1/3	one-third	*un tiers*
2/3	two-thirds	*deux tiers*
3/4	three-fourth	*trios quarts*
1/6	one-sixth	*un sixième*
1/12	one-twelfth	*un douzième*
7/12	seven-twelfths	*sept douzième*
1/100	one-hundredth	*un centième*
1/1000	one-thousandth	*un millième*

4
YOU
TU AND VOUS

In French, there are two words for "you".

1. Tu (pronounced as Tyoo)
2. Vous (pronounced as Voo)

There are two verbs *Tutoyer* and *Vouvoyer*. *Tutoyer* means to call someone *Tu,* and *Vouvoyer* means to call someone *Vous.*

1. *Vous* is the plural 'you'. It is always used when you are talking to more than one person or thing. *Tu* is never used in the plural form.

2. *Vous* can be used in the singular form to show respect or maintain a certain distance from a person. *Vous* is used when speaking to

    a person you don't know well
    a person you want to show respect to
    an older person
    a person with authority

Tu is used in the singular form to show a certain closeness and informality. *Tu* is used when speaking to just one person whom you know well.

    a friend
    a relative
    a colleague
    a child
    a pet

5

ARTICLES
ARTICLES

INDEFINITE ARTICLES
LES ARTICLES INDÉFINIS

In French, there are three indefinite articles

UN	masculine singular
UNE	feminine singular
DES	plural

UN and UNE can be translated as **a** or **an** in English. DES can be translated either as **some** or can be left untranslated.

un livre	a book
un stylo	a pen
un crayon	a pencil
une table	a table
une porte	a door
une chaise	a chair
une horloge	a clock
un oiseau	a bird
une tègle	a scale
une gomme	an eraser

une serviette	a briefcase
un bureau	an office
un taille-crayon	a sharpner
un dossier	a file
une voiture	a car
une fleur	a flower
un journal	a newspaper
un radio	a radio
une télévision	a television
un film	a film
des garçons	boys
des filles	girls
des hommes	men
des femmes	women
des oeufs	eggs

Expressions

Qu'est-ce que c'est ?
What is this ?

C'est une horloge.
This is a clock.

C'est un fauteuil.
This is an armchair

Ce sont des fauteuils.
These are armchairs.

Qui est-ce ?
Who is this ?

C'est une fille.
This is a girl.

C'est un garçon.
This is a boy.

Ce sont des parents.
These are parents.

DEFINITE ARTICLES
LES ARTICLES DÉFINIS

In French, there are four definite articles.

LE	masculine singular
LA	feminine singular
L'	vowels (a, e, i, o, u & sometimes h)
LES	plural

All the four definite articles can be translated as *the* in English.

la calculatrice	the calculator
la trousse	the pencil-case
le stylo à bille	the ball-point pen
l'ordinateur	the computer
la platine-laser	the CD player
le cahier	the notebook

l'agenda	the diary
la boîte	the box
les amis (m)	the friends
les lits (m)	the beds
les lampes (f)	the lamps
le frère	the brother
l'animal	the animal
la couleur	the colour
la musique	the music

Expressions

This is Diego's watch.
C'est la montre de Diego.

This is Robert's house.
C'est la maison de Robert.

These are Mr. Martin's sons.
Ce sont les fils de M. Martin.

6

PRESENTATION
PRESENTATION

PRESENT YOURSELF
PRESENTEZ-VOUS

My name is Diego.
Je m'appelle Diego.

I am 10 years old.
J'ai dix ans.

I live in India, in New Delhi.
J' habite en Inde, à New Delhi.

I am an Indian.
Je suis Indien (ne).

I am a student.
Je suis étudiant (e).

I work with IBM.
Je travaille à l' IBM.

I speak Hindi, English and French.
Je parle hindi, anglais et français.

I am vegetarian.
Je suis végétarien.

PRESENT A THIRD PERSON (MASCULINE)

His name is Diego.
Il s'appelle Diego.

He is 24 years old.
Il a Vingt-quatre ans.

He lives in France, in Lyon.
Il habite en France, à Lyon.

He is French.
Il est français.

He is a businessman.
Il est homme d'affaires.

He works with Indicaa Global.
Il travaille à Indicaa Global.

He speaks Spanish and French.
Il parle espagnol et français.

PRESENT A THIRD PERSON (FEMININE)

Her name is Roshini.
Elle s'appelle Roshini.

She is 20 years old.
Elle a vingt ans.

She is American.
Elle est américaine.

She is a housewife.
Elle est femme au foyer.

She lives in U.S.A., in New York.
Elle habite aux États-Unis, à New York.

She speaks Italian and Chinese.
Elle parle italien et chinois.

7

SALUTATIONS AND EXPRESSIONS
SALUTATIONS ET EXPRESSIONS

Good morning.
Bonjour.

Good afternoon.
Bon après-midi.

Good evening.
Bonsoir.

Good night.
Bonne nuit.

Hi / Hello !
Salut !

Yes.
Oui.

No.
Non.

Please.
S'il vous plaît.

Thank you.
Merci.

Sorry.
Désolée.

Welcome.
De rien.

Excuse me.
Excusez-moi.

Pardon.
Pardon.

Goodbye.
Au Revoir.

See you tommorow.
À Demain.

Never mind.
Ça ne fait rien !

Congratulations.
Felicitations !

Happy journey !
Bon voyage !

Have a good meal !
Bon appetit !

Please repeat.
Répétez, s'il vous plaît.

See you soon.
À bientôt.

That's enough.
C'est marre !

26

I have had enough of you.
J'en ai marre de toi !

Have a seat.
Asseyez-vous.

Please come in.
Entrez, s'il vous plaît.

Be careful !
Attention !

Wait.
Attendez.

How are you ? (Formal)
Comment allez-vaus ?

How are you ? (Informal)
Comment vas-tu ?

I am fine, thank you.
Je vais bien, merci.

How are things going ?
Ça Va ?

Everything is fine.
Ça Va bien.

What is your name ? (Formal)
Comment vous appelez-vous ?

What is your name ? (Informal)
Comment tu t'appelles ?

My name is Robert.
Je m'appelle Robert.

How old are you ? (Formal)
Quel âge avez-vous ?

How old are you ? (Informal)
Quel âge as-tu ?

I am 10 years old.
J'ai 10 ans.

Where do you live ? (Formal)
Où habitez-vous ?

Where do you live ? (Informal)
Où habites-tu ?

I live in Paris.
J'habite à Paris.

What is your nationality ? (Formal)
Quelle est votre nationalité ?

What is your nationality ? (Informal)
Quelle est ta nationalité ?

I am an Indian.
Je suis Indien (Masc.).
Je suis Indienne (fém).

I come from India.
Je viens d' Inde.

You come from which country ?
Vous venez de quel pays ?

Are you married ?
Vous êtes marié ?

Yes, I am married.
Oui, je suis marié.

No, I am a bachelor / spinster.
Non, je suis célibataire.

I have two children.
J'ai deux enfants.

What does this mean ?
Qu'est-ce que cela veut dire ?

Can you speak French ?
Parlez-vous français.

I can speak a little French.
Je parle un peu français.

Can you speak English ?
Parlez-vous anglais ?

Are you busy ?
Êtes-vous occupé ?

I am free.
Je suis libre.

I am busy.
Je suis occupé.

Do you smoke ?
Vous fumez ?

What are you doing ?
Que faites-vous ? ·

What does your father do ?
Que fait ton père ?

What does your mother do ?
Que fait ta mère ?

Glad to know you.
Enchanté de faire votre connaissance.

I/we'd like to.
Je voudrais / Nous voudrions.

Can I / Can we ?
Puis-je / Pouvons-nous ?

There is / There are
Il y a

There isn't / aren't
Il n'y a pas.

Now
Maintenant

Later
Plus tard

Before
Avant

After
Après

Always
Toujours

Never
Jamais

Sometimes
De temps en temps

Often
Souvent

Then
Ensuite

Enough
Assez de

Lots of
Beaucoup de

All
Tous

Everybody
Tout le monde

Nobody
Personne

Everywhere
Partout

Nowhere
Nulle part

Everything
Tout

Nothing
Rien

Something
Quelque chose

8

DAYS AND MONTHS
LES JOURS ET LES MOIS

THE DAYS OF THE WEEK
LES JOURS DE LA SEMAINE

Monday	*Lundi*
Tuesday	*Mardi*
Wednesday	*Mercredi*
Thursday	*Jeudi*
Friday	*Vendredi*
Saturday	*Samedi*
Sunday	*Dimanche*

THE MONTHS OF THE YEAR
LES MOIS DE L'ANNÉE

January	*Janvier*
February	*Février*
March	*Mars*
April	*Avril*
May	*Mai*
June	*Juin*

July	*Juillet*
August	*Août*
September	*Septembre*
October	*Octobre*
November	*Novembre*
December	*Décembre*

9

TIME AND DATE
L'HEURE ET LA DATE

TIME
L'HEURE

Vocabulary

A watch	*Une montre*
A clock	*Une horloge*
A hand	*Une aiguille*
The minutes hand	*L'aiguille des minutes*
The seconds hand	*L'aiguille des secondes*
The hour hand	*L'aiguille des heures*
Numbers	*Des chiffres*
A dial	*Un cadran*
An hour	*Une heure*
A minute	*Une minute*
A second	*Une seconde*
Morning	*Matin*
Afternoon	*Après-midi*
Evening	*Soir*
Night	*Nuit*

Sun	Soleil
Moon	Lune
Stars	Des étoiles
The sky	Le ciel
Clouds	Des nuages

Expressions

What is the time ?
Quelle heure est-il ?

At what time ?
À quelle heure ?

On time
à l'heure

late
en retard

before time
en avance

24.00/00:00 It is midnight	*Il est minuit*
01:00 It is 1 o'clock	*Il est une heure*
02:00 It is 2 o'clock	*Il est deux heures*
03:00 It is 3 o'clock	*Il est trois heures*
12:00 It is noon	*Il est midi*
13:00 It is 1 p.m.	*Il est treize heures* *Il est une heure de l'après-midi*

15:00	It is 3 p.m.	*Il est quinze heures*
		Il est trois heures de l'après-midi
06:30	It is six thirty	*Il est six heures et demie*
	It is half past six	
06:15	It is six fifteen	*Il est six heures quinze*
	It is quarter past six	*Il est six heures et quart.*
6:45	It is six forty-five	*Il est six heures quarante cinq*
	It is quarter to seven	*Il est sept heures moins le quart*
6:10	It is ten past six	*Il est six heures dix*
6:50	It is six fifty	*Il est six heures cinquante*
	It is ten to seven	*Il est sept heures moins dix*

DATE
LA DATE

Vocabulary

A day	*Un jour*
A week	*Une semaine*
A fortnight	*Une quinzaine*
A month	*Un mois*
A year	*Une année*
Day before yesterday	*Avant-hier*
Yesterday	*Hier*
Today	*Aujourd' hui*

Tomorrow	*Demain*
Day after tomorrow	*Après-demain*
Last week	*La Semaine dernière*
Next week	*La Semaine prochaine*
Last month	*Le mois dernier*
Next month	*Le mois prochain*
Last year	*L'année dernière*
Next year	*L'année prochaine*

In French the date is always preceded by the definite article *Le*. So, to write the date, use le + the number + the month.

> *le 8 juin* 2003

But if it is the first of a month, use premier instead of 1.

> *le premier mars* 2004

But if the day is also mentioned, one can omit the le.

> *Jeudi 8 juin* 2003

What is the date today ?
Quelle est la date d'aujourd'hui ?

This question can be answered in two ways.

Aujourd'hui nous sommes le 27 mars 2003.
Aujourd'hui c'est le 27 mars 2003.

To refer to a year, use the preposition *EN*.

> In 1848
> *En* 1848

To refer to a month, use the preposition *EN* on we write *AU MOIS DE*

> In January
> *En janvier*

> In the month of January
> *Au mois de janvier.*

10

THE COLOURS
LES COULEURS

Of which colour is ... ?
De Quelle couleur est ... ?

	Masculine	Feminine	M. Pl.	Fém. Pl.
Red	*Rouge*	*Rouge*	*Rouges*	*Rouges*
Blue	*Bleu*	*Bleue*	*Bleus*	*Bleues*
Green	*Vert*	*Verte*	*Verts*	*Vertes*
Yellow	*Jaune*	*Jaune*	*Jaunes*	*Jaunes*
Orange	*Orange*	*Orange*	*Oranges*	*Oranges*
Purple	*Violet*	*Violette*	*Violets*	*Violettes*
White	*Blanc*	*Blanche*	*Blancs*	*Blanches*
Black	*Noir*	*Noire*	*Noirs*	*Noires*
Grey	*Gris*	*Grise*	*Gris*	*Grises*
Brown	*Brun*	*Brune*	*Bruns*	*Brunes*
Pink	*Rose*	*Rose*	*Roses*	*Roses*
Maroon	*Marron*	*Marronne*	*Marrons*	*Marronnes*
Sky blue	*bleu ciel*	*bleu ciel*	*bleu ciel*	*bleu ciel*
Light blue	*bleu clair*	*bleu clair*	*bleu clair*	*bleu clair*
Dark blue	*bleu foncé*	*bleu foncé*	*bleu foncé*	*bleu foncé*
Blond	*blond*	*blonde*	*blonds*	*blondes*
Turquoise	*turquoise*	*turquoise*	*turquoises*	*turquoises*

Unlike in English, the colours in French change to agree in gender and number with the noun.

The pronunciation of the colours is the same in singular and plural form.

Using the modifiers, dark (*foncé*) and light (*clair*), makes the colour invariable. It does not change to agree in number or gender.

The colours are always placed after the noun. For example,

a green book.
un livre vert.

11

VERBS
LES VERBES

There are three groups of verbs in French, which are determined by the endings of the verbs. But before classifying these verbs we need to see their infinitive form, from which we derive their conjugated form. The verbs in the infinitive form are called so because they are not bound by time. The infinitive form is English is preceded by the word 'to'.

to eat	*manger*
to sleep	*dormir*
to learn	*apprendre*

We conjugate these verbs in accordance with time, i.e. in the present, past or the future tense.

All regular verbs can be divided into three groups based on the ending, i.e. the last two letters of the verb. The first group consists of verbs ending in 'ER', the second group consists of those ending in 'IR' and the third in 'RE'.

Verbs are generally conjugated in six forms, according to the subjects. Every verb form begins with a pronoun.

Je	I
Tu	You (singular and informal)

{ Il	He
Elle	She
Nous	We
Vous	You (Singular formal and plural)
{ Ils	They (masculine)
Elles	They (feminine)

The conjugation in the *'il'* and *'elle'* form and in the *'ils'* and *'elles'* form is always the same.

To memorise the conjugation of a verb, you only need to memorise the endings because the stem of the verb normally remains the same.

For example, the verb *'Parler'* is in the infinitive form. 'ER' is the ending of the verb and the beginning *'Parl'* is the stem. The endings of 'er' verbs are as follows :

Parler (To speak)

Je	e	*parle*	I speak
Tu	es	*parles*	You speak
Il	e	*parle*	He speaks
Elle	e	*parle*	She speaks
Nous	ons	*parlons*	We speak
Vous	ez	*parlez*	You speak
Ils	ent	*parlent*	They speak (m)
Elles	ent	*parlent*	They speak (f)

43

chanter (To sing)

Je chante	I sing
Tu chantes	You sing
Il chante	He sings
Elle chante	She sings
Nous chantons	We sing
Vous chantez	You sing
Ils chantent	They sing (m)
Elles chantent	They sing (f)

Sometimes the 'er' verbs undergo a change to facilitate the pronunciation.

The verbs ending in 'ger', for example. We add an 'e' before 'ons' and after 'g' to give the soft sound in the 'nous' form. For example,

Manger (To eat)

Je mange	I eat
Tu manges	You eat
Il mange	He eats
Elle mange	She eats
Nous mangeons	We eat
Vous mangez	You eat
Ils mangent	They eat (m)
Elles mangent	They eat (f)

44

Similarly, in case of verbs ending in 'cer', it is necessary to add cedille to the letter c, i.e., to change it to ç before 'ons' in the nous form, to give it a soft sound.

Commencer (To start)

Je commence	I start
Tu commences	You start
Il commence	He starts
Elle commence	She starts
Nous commençons	We start
Vous commencez	You start
Ils commencent	They start (m)
Elles commencent	They start (f)

Sometimes there are changes in the accents of the verb while conjugating it.

Préférer (To prefer)

Je préfère	I prefer
Tu préfères	You prefer
Il préfère	He prefers
Elle préfère	She prefers
Nous préférons	We prefer
Vous préférez	You prefer
Ils préfèrent	They prefer (m)
Elles préfèrent	They prefer (f)

45

The second group of verbs is those that end in 'IR'. For example, *finir* (to finish), *grossir* (to become fat), etc.

Finir (To finish)

Je	is	*finis*	I finish
Tu	is	*finis*	You finish
Il	it	*finit*	He finishes
Elle	it	*finit*	She finishes
Nous	issons	*finissons*	We finish
Vous	issez	*finissez*	You finish
Ils	issent	*finissent*	They finish (m)
Elles	issent	*finissent*	They finish (f)

Grossir (To become fat)

Je grossis	I become fat
Tu grossis	You become fat
Il grossit	He becomes fat
Elle grossit	She becomes fat
Nous grossissons	We become fat
Vous grossissez	You become fat
Ils grossissent	They become fat (m)
Elles grossissent	They become fat (f)

The third group of verbs is those that end in 'RE'. For example, *prendre* (to take), *boire* (to drink). The verbs in the third group usually don't have any fixed pattern.

Prendre (To take)

Je prends	I take
Tu prends	You take
Il prend	He takes
Elle prend	She takes
Nous prenons	We take
Vous prenez	You take
Ils prennent	They take (m)
Elles prennent	They take (f)

Boire (To drink)

Je bois	I drink
Tu bois	You drink
Il boit	He drinks
Elle boit	She drinks
Nous buvons	We drink
Vous buvez	You drink
Ils boivent	They drink (m)
Elles boivent	They drink (f)

There are other irregular verbs whose conjugations are very important.

Être (To be)

Je suis	I am
Tu es	You are
Il est	He is
Elle est	She is
Nous sommes	We are
Vous êtes	You are
Ils sont	They are (m)
Elles sont	They are (f)

Avoir (To have)

J'ai	I have
Tu as	You have
Il a	He has
Elle a	She has
Nous avons	We have
Vous avez	You have
Ils ont	They have (m)
Elles ont	They have (f)

Aller (To go)

Je vais	I go
Tu vas	You go
Il va	He goes

Elle va	She goes
Nous allons	We go
Vous allez	You go
Ils vont	They go (m)
Elles vont	They go (f)

Venir (To come)

Je viens	I come
Tu viens	You come
Il vient	He comes
Elle vient	She comes
Nous venons	We come
Vous venez	You come
Ils viennent	They come (m)
Elles viennent	They come (f)

Faire (To do/To make)

Je fais	I do/make
Tu fais	You do/make
Il fait	He does/makes
Elle fait	She does/makes
Nous faisons	We do/make
Vous faites	You do/make
Ils font	They do/make (m)
Elles font	They do/make (f)

Pouvoir (To be able to)

Je peux	I can
Tu peux	You can
Il peut	He can
Elle peut	She can
Nous pouvons	We can
Vous pouvez	You can
Ils peuvent	They can (m)
Elles peuvent	They can (f)

Vouloir (To want)

Je veux	I want
Tu veux	You want
Il veut	He wants
Elle veut	She wants
Nous voulons	We want
Vous voulez	You want
Ils veulent	They want (m)
Elles veulent	They want (f)

12

FUTURE TENSE
LE FUTUR

In the future tense, we add the following endings to the verb in the infinitive directly if it is an *'ER'* verb or *IR* verb. We remove the R and then add the endings if it is an *RE* verb.

Regarder (To watch)

Je regarderai	ai	I will watch
Tu regarderas	as	You will watch
Il regardera	a	He will watch
Elle regardera	a	She will watch
Nous regardons	ons	We will watch
Vous regarderez	ez	You will watch
Ils regarderont	ont	They will watch (m)
Elles regarderont	ont	They will watch (f)

Partir (To leave)

Je partirai	I will leave
Tu partiras	You will leave
Il partira	He will leave
Elle partira	She will leave
Nous partirons	We will leave
Vous partirez	You will leave
Ils partiront	They will leave (m)
Elles partiront	They will leave (f)

Dire (To say)

Je dirai	I will say
Tu diras	You will say
Il dira	He will say
Elle dira	She will say
Nous dirons	We will say
Vous direz	You will say
Ils diront	They will say (m)
Elles diront	They will say (f)

However, there are certain exceptions.

Venir	*Je viendrai*	I will come
Aller	*J'irai*	I will go
Être	*Je serai*	I will be
Avoir	*J'aurai*	I will have
Faire	*Je ferai*	I will do
Vouloir	*Je voudrai*	I will want
Pouvoir	*Je pourrai*	I will be able to
Savoir	*Je saurai*	I will know
Voir	*Je verrai*	I will see
Devoir	*Je devrai*	I would have to
Courrir	*Je courrai*	I will run
Mourir	*Je mourrai*	I will die

13

PAST TENSE
LE PASSÉ COMPOSÉ

To form the past tense, we can use the following formula :

Subject + auxiliary verb + past participle of the verb

The auxiliary verb in French can either be *'être'* or *'avoir'*. The following fifteen verbs, and all pronominal/ reflexive verbs, take *'être'* as the auxiliary verb. All the others take *avoir*.

arriver	to arrive
partir	to leave
descendre	to descend
monter	to climb
venir	to come
aller	to go
entrer	to enter
sortir	to go out
naître	to be born
mourir	to die
tomber	to fall
retourner	to return
passer	to pass
rester	to stay
devenir	to become

The past participle of 'er' verbs is formed by removing the 'r' from the end and putting an accent aigu ´ on the last 'e'.

For example : *Parler*

Remove 'r', i.e. *parle*.

Add the accent, i.e. *parlé*.

Add the past participle of the verb Parler, i.e. *parlé*.

> *J'ai parlé.*
> I spoke.

The past participle of 'IR' verbs is simply made by removing the 'r' from the end.

For example : *Finir*

Thus, the past participle is *fini*.

e.g., *J'ai fini.*
> I finished.

For all others, one must learn their past participles.

Verb	Past participle	
être	*été*	was
avoir	*eu*	had
faire	*fait*	did
venir	*venu*	came
aller	*allé*	went
sortir	*sorti*	left
naître	*né*	born

mourir	*mort*	died
ouvrir	*ouvert*	opened
couvrir	*couvert*	covered
boire	*bu*	drank
voir	*vu*	saw
lire	*lu*	read
dire	*dit*	said
recevoir	*reçu*	received
mettre	*mis*	put
prendre	*pris*	took
apprendre	*appris*	learnt
comprendre	*compris*	understood
S'asseoir	*assis*	sat
attendre	*attendu*	waited
battre	*battu*	beat
choisir	*choisi*	chose
conduire	*conduit*	drove
connaître	*connu*	knew
construire	*construit*	constructed
descendre	*descendu*	descended
entendre	*entendu*	heard
courir	*couru*	ran
croire	*cru*	believed

découvrir	*découvert*	discovered
devenir	*devenu*	became
dormir	*dormi*	slept
écrire	écrit	wrote
falloir	fallu	must
offrir	offert	offered
peindre	peint	painted
pouvoir	pu	could
vouloir	voulu	wanted
pleuvoir	plu	rained
perdre	perdu	lost
permettre	permis	allowed
produire	produit	produced
reconnaître	reconnu	recognised
rendre	rendu	returned
répondre	répondu	answered
rire	ri	laughed
savoir	su	knew
sentir	senti	felt/smelt
suivre	suivi	followed
vendre	vendu	sold
vivre	vécu	lived

14

NEAR FUTURE
LE FUTUR PROCHE

The *futur proche* is used to show the near future, i.e. when an action is going to take place in a very short period of time. It is used with the verb *aller* (to go). The following formula is used :

Subject + aller + verb (in the infinitive form)

Example :   I am going to eat.
Je vais manger.

She is going to see a film.
Elle va voir un film.

Thus, proche can be further translated as 'going to' in English.

The *negative* form of *'futur proche'* is formed by adding *NE* or *N'* (if the next word starts with a vowel) before the verb *'aller'* and PAS after the verb *'aller'*.

For example :

I am not going to drink water.
Je ne vais pas boire d'eau.

We are not going to talk to Diego.
Nous n'allons pas parler à Diego.

The interrogative form of *'futur proche'* is formed by interrogating/inverting the verb *'aller'* with the subject.

For example :

Is he going to go to Africa ?
Va-t-il aller en Afrique ?

Are you going to stay without him in France ?
Vas-tu rester sans lui en France ?

15

RECENT PAST
PASSÉ RÉCENT

The *'Passé Récent'* is used to show an action that took place in the recent past. It is formed with the verb *'venir'* (to come). This tense can be translated in English as 'just'. It is formed according to the following formula :

Subject + venir + de + verb (in the infinitive form)

Example :

He just wrote a letter
Il vient d'écrire une lettre.

De changes to D' before a vowel.

We just ate our dinner
Nous venons de prendre notre dîner.

The negative form of **'Passé Récent'** is formed by putting Ne before the verb *'venir'* and *'Pas'* after the verb *'venir'*.

For example :

He didn't just write the letter.
Il ne vient pas d'écrire la letter.

We didn't just send you the card.
Nous ne venons pas de t'envoyer la carte.

The interrogative form of *'Passé Récent'* is formed by inverting the verb *'venir'* with the subject.

For example :

Did he just call you ?
Vient-il de t'appeler ?

Did Diego just leave his country ?
Diego, vient-il de quitter son pays ?

16

COUNTRIES AND NATIONALITIES
PAYS ET NATIONALITÉS

COUNTRIES
LES PAYS

Unlike in English, all the countries have a gender. They are either masculine or feminine. All the countries ending with the letter 'e' are feminine. However, there are some exceptions. *Mexique* (Mexico), *Zaïre* (Zaire) and *Madagascar* (Madagascar). These countries end with an 'e' but are masculine. All the countries carry a definite article.

> *Ex.* France is a beautiful country.
> *La France est un beau pays.*

The countries take prepositions according to their number and their gender.

The countries that are plural, take AUX.

> *Ex.* He lives in United States of America.
> *Il habite **aux** États-Unis.*

The countries that are masculine, take AU.

> They are going to Pakistan.
> *Ils vont **au** Pakistan.*

The countries that are feminine, take EN.

> We are in China.
> *Nous sommes **en** Chine.*

The countries starting with a vowel also take EN.

I live in India with Shiv.
J'habite en Inde avec Shiv.

Vocabulary

India	*l'Inde*
France	*la France*
Japan	*le Japon*
China	*la Chine*
America	*l'Amérique*
Switzerland	*la Suisse*
England	*l'Angleterre*
Portugal	*le Portugal*
Mexico	*le Mexique*
Hungary	*le Hongrie*
Pakistan	*le Pakistan*
Zaire	*le Zaïre*
United States	*les États-Unis*
Morocco	*le Maroc*
Belgium	*la Belgique*
Spain	*l'Espagne*
Italy	*l'Italie*
Germany	*l'Allemagne*

Russia	*la Russie*
Canada	*le Canada*
Zimbabwe	*le Zimbabwe*
Sri Lanka	*le Sri Lanka*
Holand	*la Hollande*
Egypt	*l'Égypte*
Brazil	*le Brésil*
Congo	*le Congo*
Gabon	*le Gabon*
Algeria	*l'Algérie*
Tunisia	*la Tunisie*
Vietnam	*le Vietnam*
Senegal	*le Sénégal*
Nigeria	*le Niger*
Mauritania	*la Mauritanie*
Madagascar	*la Madagascar*
Cambodia	*le Cambodge*
Burkina Faso	*le Burkina Faso*
Luxembourg	*le Luxembourg*
Australia	*l'Australie*
Scotland	*l'Ecosse*
Wales	*le pays de Galles*

Ireland	*l'Irlande*
Zambia	*la Zambie*
Austria	*l'Autriche*
Mauritius	*la Maurice*
Burma	*la Birmanie*

NATIONALITIES
LES NATIONALITÉS

The nationalities in French also change according to the number and gender. For example

> a French boy
> *un garçon français*

> a French girl
> *une fille française.*

Thus, we generally add 'e' at the end of the nationality to change it to feminine, and an 's' to change it to plural. For example,

> an Indian boy
> *un garçon indien.*

> Indian boys
> *des garçons indiens.*

But if there is an 'e' or an 's' already at the end, we don't make any changes. For example,

> a French boy
> *un garçon français*

French boys
des garçons français

a Swiss boy
un garçon suisse.

a Swiss girl
une fille suisse

Nationality	Masculine Form	Feminine Form
Indian	*indien*	*indienne*
French	*français*	*française*
Japanese	*japonais*	*japonaise*
Chinese	*chinois*	*chinoise*
American	*américain*	*américaine*
Swiss	*suisse*	*suisse*
English	*anglais*	*anglaise*
Portuguese	*portugais*	*portugaise*
Mexican	*mexicain*	*mexicaine*
Hungarian	*hongrois*	*hongroise*
Pakistani	*pakistanais*	*pakistanaise*
Zairean	*zaïrois*	*zaïroise*
Moroccan	*marocain*	*marocaine*
Belgian	*belge*	*belge*
Spanish	*espagnol*	*espagnole*
Italian	*italien*	*italienne*

German	*allemand*	*allemande*
Russian	*russe*	*russe*
Canadian	*canadien*	*canadienne*
Sri Lankan	*srilankais*	*srilankaise*
Egyptian	*égyptien*	*égyptiennne*
Brazilian	*brésilien*	*brésilienne*
Algerian	*algérien*	*algérienne*
Tunisian	*tunisien*	*tunisienné*
Senegalese	*sénégalais*	*sénégalaise*
Nigerian	*nigérian*	*nigériane*
Australian	*australien*	*australienne*
Irish	*irlandais*	*irlandaise*
Zambian	*zambien*	*zambienne*
Zimbabwean	*zimbabwéen*	*zimbabwéenne*
Austrian	*autrichien*	*autrichienne*
Congolese	*congolais*	*congolaise*
Gabonese	*gabonais*	*gabonaise*
Mauritanian	*mauritanien*	*mauritanienne*
Mauritian	*mauricien*	*mauricienne*
Madagascan	*malgache*	*malgache*
Cambodian	*cambodgien*	*cambodgienne*
Burmese	*birman*	*birmane*
Scottish	*écossais*	*écossaise*

17

SEASONS
SAISONS

Vocabulary

The season	*La saison*
summer	*L'été*
autumn	*L'automne*
winter	*L'hiver*
spring	*Le printemps*
in summers	*en été*
in autumn	*en automne*
in winters	*en hiver*
in spring	*au printemps*

Expressions

Quel temps fait-il ?
How is the weather ?

Il pleut.
It rains / It is raining.

Il fait du soleil.
It is sunny.

Le soleil brille.
The sun is shining.

Il neige / Il y a de la neige.
It snows / It is snowing.

La neige tombe.
The snow falls / The snow is falling

Il fait du vent.
It is windy

Il fait chaud.
It is hot.

Il fait foid.
It is cold.

Il fait beau.
It is pleasant.

Il fait mauvais.
It is bad weather.

Il y a du brouillard.
It is foggy.

To describe the weather, we use the verb *"faire"* with the impersonal pronoun "it", instead of the verb *"être"* (which means 'to be').

18

CONTRACTED ARTICLES
ARTICLES CONTRACTÉS

As the name suggests, the definite articles and the prepositions A and DE contract to form the contracted articles.

The preposition À means to / at / in

> *Elle va à Paris*
> She goes to Paris

> *Elle est à Delhi*
> She is in Delhi

We have already studied the definite articles.

Le	(masc.) sing
La	(fem.) sing
L'	vowels
Les	plural

which mean 'The'.

The preposition À and the definite articles contract in the following manner to form contracted articles :

À + le → Au

À + la → À la

À + l' → À l'

À + les → Aux

These can be translated as 'to the', 'at the', or 'in the'.

> She goes to the market.
> *Elle va (à + le) au marché.*

> He goes to the station.
> *Il va (à + la) à la gare.*

> We are at the airport.
> *Nous sommes (à + l') à l'aéroport.*

> They go to the schools
> *Ils vont (à + les) aux écoles.*

Similarly, the preposition DE means 'of' or 'from'

> He is coming from Paris.
> *Il vient de Paris.*

> He is coming from Agra.
> *Il vient d'Agra.*

DE changes to *D´* before a vowel.

The preposition *DE* and the definite articles contract in the following manner to form contracted articles :

> *De + le → Du*
>
> *De + la → De la*
>
> *De + l' → Del'*
>
> *De + les → Des*

which can be translated as 'of the' or 'from the'.

I come from the church
Je viens (de + l') de l' église

She is coming from the house.
Elle vient (de + la) de la maison.

We are coming from the shops.
Nous venons (de + les) des magasins.

Vocabulary

the church	*l'église*
the shop	*le magasin*
the market	*le marché*
the house	*la maison*
the cinema	*le cinéma*
the theatre	*le théâtre*
the hotel	*l'hôtel*
the school	*l'école*
the airport	*l'aéroport*
the station	*la gare*
the bank	*la banque*
the bakery	*la boulangerie*
the office	*le bureau*
the hospital	*l'hôpital*
the park	*le parc*
the garden	*le jardin*

the swimming pool	*la piscine*
the cafe	*le café*
the museum	*le musée*
the opera	*l'opéra*
the disco	*le discothéque*
the post office	*la poste*
the cathedral	*la cathédrale*
the supermarket	*le supermarché*
the beach	*la plage*
the restaurant	*le restaurant*
the farm	*la ferme*
the campsite	*le camping*
the tower	*la tour*
the square	*la place*

19

FACE AND BODY
VISAGE ET CORPS

THE FACE
LE VISAGE

Vocabulary

an eye	*un oeil*
eyes	*des yeux*
a nose	*un nez*
a lip	*une lèvre*
a chin	*un menton*
a cheek	*une joue*
an ear	*une oreille*
an eyebrow	*un cil*
hair	*des cheveux*
moustache	*une moustache*
beard	*une barbre*
a tooth	*un dent*
a tongue	*une langue*
a head	*une tête*
a mouth	*une bouche*

a forehead	*un front*
a skull	*un crâne*
a brain	*un cerveau*
an eyeball	*un globe*
an eyelid	*une paupière*
a gum	*une gencive*
a jaw	*une mâchoire*
a throat	*une gorge*
a jawbone	*un maxillaire*

THE BODY
LE CORPS

a limb	*un membre*
an arm	*un bras*
a hand	*une main*
a finger	*un doigt*
a nail	*une ongle*
a leg	*une jamble*
a foot	*un pied*
a neck	*un cou*
a shoulder	*une épaule*
an elbow	*un coude*
a knee	*un genou*

a back	*un dos*
a stomach	*un ventre*
a chest	*une poitrine*
a collarbone	*une clavicule*
a lung	*un poumon*
a heart	*un coeur*
blood	*sang*
an artery	*une artère*
a muscle	*un muscle*
a windpipe	*une trachée*
a breast	*un sein, une mamelle*
a rib	*une côte*
a spine	*une colonne vertébrale*
an upper arm	*un haut du bras*
a waist	*une taille*
an abdomen	*un abdomen*
an intestine	*un intestin*
a kidney	*un rein*
a liver	*un foie*
a uterus	*un utérus*
a gall bladder	*une vésicule biliaire*
a urinary bladder	*une vessie*

a nerve	*un nerf*
a forearm	*un avant-bras*
a navel	*un nombril*
a thumb	*un pouce*
an index finger	*un index*
a middle finger	*un majeur*
a ring finger	*un annulaire*
a little finger	*un petit doigt*
a palm	*une paume*
a wrist	*un poignet*
buttocks	*des fesses*
a pelvis	*un pelvis*
a thigh	*une cuisse*
a thigh bone	*un fémur*
a knee cap	*une rotule*
a lower leg	*une partie inférieure de la jambe*
a calf	*un mollet*
an ankle	*une cheville*
an instep	*un cou de pied*
a sole	*une plante*
a toe	*un doigt de pied*
a heel	*un talon*

20

PREPOSITIONS
PRÉPOSITIONS

to, at, in — *à*

I speak to Robert.
Je parle à Robert.

He is at the hotel.
Il est à l'hôtel.

He is in Delhi.
Il est à Delhi.

next to, beside — *à côté de*

She is sitting next to the boy.
Elle est assise à côté du garçon.

after — *après*

I am going to come after the party.
Je vais venir après la soirée.

about, on the subject of — *au sujet de*

The professor is speaking about politics.
Le professeur parle au sujet de la politique.

before — *avant*

The girl will eat before her father.
La fille mangera avant son père.

with — *avec*

He goes to the pool with his wife.
Il va à la piscine avec sa femme.

at the home/office of — *chez*

He returns to his brother's home.
Il rentre chez son frère.

against — *contre*

The picture is against the wall.
L'image est contre le mur.

in — *dans*

The pen is in the bag.
Le stylo est dans le sac.

according to — *d'après*

According to Peter, one must not smoke.
D'après Pierre, il ne faut pas fumer.

from, of, about — *de*

He comes from Delhi.
Il vient de Delhi.

The bag is made of cloth.
Le sac est d'étoffe.

He speaks about the party.
Il parle de la soirée.

since, for — *depuis*

He has been working in the office for 5 years.
Il travaille dans le bureau depuis 5 ans.

Behind — *derrière*

> The garden is behind the house.
> *Le jardin est derrière la maison.*

in front of — *devant*

> The car is in front of the house.
> *La voiture est devant la maison.*

during, while — *durant*

> It rained during the night.
> *Il a plu durant la nuit.*

in — *en*

> He is in Europe.
> *Il est en Europe.*

outside — *en dehors de*

> The dog stays outside the room.
> *Le chien reste en dehors de la chambre.*

facing, across from — *en face de*

> The hospital is facing my villa.
> *L'hôpital est en face de ma villa.*

between — *entre*

> Sit between those two boys.
> *Asseyez-vous entre ces deux garçons.*

towards — *envers*

> His attitude towards his mother is not good.
> *Son attitude envers sa mère n'est pas bonne.*

approximately — *environ*

The room is approximately 15 metres high.
La chambre a environ 15 mètres de haut.

outside of — *hors de*

He stays outside the town.
Il habite hors de la ville.

uptil, upto, even — *jusque*

The children stay in this school up to the age of 5 years.
Les enfants restent dans cette école jusqu'à l'âge de 5 ans.

far from — *loin de*

He lives far from the station.
Il habite loin de la gare.

despite — *malgré*

He went out despite the bad weather.
Il est sorti malgré le mauvais temps.

by, through — *par*

I saw through the window.
J'ai vu par la fenêtre.

among — *parmi*

He chose one house among the others.
Il a choisi une maison parmi les autres.

during — *pendant*

He taught during 9 days.
Il a enseigné pendant 9 jours.

for — *pour*

> I study for the exam.
> *J'étudie pour l'examen.*

near — *près*

> The table is near the door.
> *La table est près de la porte.*

as for, regarding — *quant à*

> As for me, I am leaving.
> *Quant à moi, je pars.*

without — *Sans*

> I don't leave without Diego.
> *Je ne pars pas sans Diego.*

according to — *selon*

> According to Ciri, one must not smoke.
> *Selon Ciri, it ne faut pas fumer.*

under — *sous*

> The cat is under the bed.
> *Le chat est sous le lit.*

on — *sur*

> The book is on the table.
> *Le livre est sur la table.*

21

POSSESSIVE ADJECTIVES AND PRONOUNS
ADJECTIFS ET PRONOMS POSSESSIFS

POSSESSIVE ADJECTIVES
LES ADJECTIFS POSSESSIFS

Unlike in English, the possessive adjectives change according to the gender, number and starting letter of the object.

	Plural	Vowel	Feminine	Masculine	
Je	*mes*	*mon*	*ma*	*mon*	my
Tu	*tes*	*ton*	*ta*	*ton*	your
Il	*ses*	*son*	*sa*	*son*	his
Elle	*ses*	*son*	*sa*	*son*	her
Noun	*nos*	*notre*	*notre*	*notre*	our
Ils	*leurs*	*leur*	*leur*	*leur*	their
Elles	*leurs*	*leur*	*leur*	*leur*	their

For Example

This is my book.
*C'est **mon** livre.*

We chose '*mon*' because the word '*livre*' is masculine.

> This is my car.
> *C'est **ma** voiture.*

We put '*ma*' because the word '*voiture*' is feminine

> These are your dolls.
> *Ce sont **tes** poupées.*

We put '*tes*' because the subject is '*tu*' and the object is in plural.

> Where is your clock ?
> *Où est **ton** horloge ?*

We put *ton* here because it starts with a vowel even though it is feminine.

When the object is in the plural form, it doesn't matter whether it is masculine, feminine or starts with a vowel. For example,

> Here are their birds.
> *Voici **leurs** oiseaux.*

POSSESSIVE PRONOUNS
LES PRONOMS POSSESSIFS

Like the possessive adjectives, the possessive pronouns also change according to the gender and number of the object.

	Masc	Fem	Masc Pl.	Fem. Pl.	
Je	*le mien*	*la mienne*	*les miens*	*les miennes*	mine
Tu	*le tien*	*la tienne*	*les tiens*	*les tiennes*	yours
Il	*le sien*	*la sienne*	*les siens*	*les siennes*	his
Elle	*le sien*	*la sienne*	*les siens*	*les siennes*	hers
Nous	*le nôtre*	*la nôtre*	*les nôtres*	*les nôtres*	ours
Vous	*le vôtre*	*la vôtre*	*les vôtres*	*les vôtres*	yours
Ils	*le leur*	*la leur*	*les leurs*	*les leurs*	theirs
Elles	*le leur*	*la leur*	*les leurs*	*les leurs*	theirs

This is mine (a book).
C'est le mien.

Because book (*livre*) is masculine.

This is his (a car).
C'est la sienne.

Because car (*la voiture*) is feminine.

This is hers (a car).
C'est la sienne.

Whether the possessor is masculine or feminine, we consider the object possessed.

These are ours (children).
Ce sont les nôtres.

These are mine (books).
Ce sont les miens.

22

INTERROGATIVE ADJECTIVES AND PRONOUNS
ADJECTIFS ET PRONOMS INTERROGATIFS

INTERROGATIVE ADJECTIVES
LES ADJECTIFS INTERROGATIFS

The interrogative adjectives vary according to the gender and number of the noun.

QUEL	masculine singular
QUELLE	feminine singular
QUELS	masculine plural
QUELLES	feminine plural

Which book are you reading ?
***Quel** livre lis-tu ?*

We use the masculine singular form of the interrogative adjectives because '*livre*' (book) is masculine.

Which dress do you prefer ?
***Quelle** robe préfères-tu ?*

We use the feminine singular form of the interrogative adjectives because '*robe*' (dress) is feminine.

Which trousers do you like ?
***Quels** pantalons aimes-tu ?*

We use the masculine plural form of the interrogative adjectives because '*pantalons*' (trousers) is masculine and is in the plural form.

Which students are you teaching ?

Quelles étudiantes enseignes-tu ?

We use the feminine plural form of the interrogative adjectives because '*étudiantes*' (students) is feminine and is in the plural form.

INTERROGATIVE PRONOUNS
LES PRONOMS INTERROGATIFS

LEQUEL	masculine singular
LAQUELLE	feminine singular
LESQUELS	masculine plural
LESQUELLES	feminine plural

We have many pens. Which one do you like ?

Nous avons plusieurs stylos. **Lequel** *préfères-tu ?*

We use the pronoun '*lequel*' to replace the masculine singluar noun '*quel stylo*' (which pen).

I showed you five houses. Which one do you want to buy ?

Je vous ai montré cinq maisons. **Laquelle** *voulez vous achetez ?*

We use the pronoun '*laquelle*' to replace the feminine singular noun '*quelle maison*' (which house).

There are several books in this library. Which ones have you read ?

If y a plusieurs livres dans cette bibliotheque. Lesquels avez-vous lus ?

We use the pronoun *'lesquels'* to replace the masculine plural noun *'quels livres'* (which books).

We have dresses of all colours. Which ones do you want to buy ?

Nous avons les robes de toutes les couleurs. Lesquelles voulez-vous acheter ?

We use the pronoun *'lesquelles'* to replace the feminine plural noun *'quelles robes'* (which dresses).

23

DEMONSTRATIVE ADJECTIVES AND PRONOUNS
ADJECTIFS ET PRONOMS DÉMONSTRATIFS

DEMONSTRATIVE ADJECTIVES
LES ADJECTIFS DÉMONSTRATIFS

The following demonstrative adjectives, which can be translated as 'this' or 'these', change according to the noun that it qualifies.

CES	plural
CETTE	feminine
CET	masculine, vowel
CE	masculine, consonant

these books	*ces livres*	plural, masculine, consonant
these chairs	*ces chaises*	plural, feminine, consonant
these clocks	*ces horloges*	plural, feminine, vowel
these birds	*ces oiseaux*	plural, masculine, vowel

Thus, we see that whether the noun is masculine or feminine, whether it starts with a consonant or vowel. If it is plural we use *ces*.

| this girl | *cette fille* | feminine, consonant |
| this school | *cette école* | feminine, vowel |

Thus, whether the noun starts with a consonant or a vowel, if it is feminine we use cette.

| this man | *cet homme* | masculine, vowel |
| this bird | *cet oiseau* | masculine, vowel |

Thus, we use **cet** when the noun is masculine and starts with a vowel.

| this boy | *ce garçon* | masculine, consonant |
| this book | *ce livre* | masculine, consonant |

Thus, we use **ce** when the noun is masculine and starts with a consonant.

DEMONSTRATIVE PRONOUNS
LES PRONOMS DÉMONSTRATIFS

The following demonstrative pronouns can be translated as 'this one' or 'these ones' and 'that one' or 'those ones'.

| this one | { | *celui-ci* | masculine, singular |
| | | *celle-ci* | feminine, singular |

| these ones | { | *ceux-ci* | masculine, plural |
| | | *celles-ci* | feminine, plural |

| that one | { | *celui-là* | masculine, singular |
| | | *celle-là* | feminine, singular |

| those ones | { | *ceux-là* | masculine, plural |
| | | *celles-là* | feminine, plural |

You have many books but this one is the best.
Vous avez plusieurs livres mais celui-ci est le meilleur.

Amongst all your dresses, I like this one.
Parmi toutes vos robes, j'aime celle-ci.

Which hankerchiefs do you want to buy ?
These ones are good, but those ones are better.
Quels mouchoirs voulez-vous acheter ?
Ceux-ci sont bons, mais ceux-là sont meilleurs.

These tables are from India, and those ones from
Paris.
Ces tables sont d' Inde et celles-là de Paris.

24

INTERROGATIVE FORM
FORME INTERROGATIVE

There are three ways of forming a question.

(a) Write the sentence as it is and add a question mark at the end. For example,

> He eats bread
> *Il mange du pain.*

Forme interrogative I

> *Il mange du pain ?*
> He eats bread ?

(b) Add the expression "*Est-ce que*" (is it that) at the beginning of the sentence and add the question mark at the end.

> You are in the cinéma.
> *Tu es au cinéma.*

Forme interrogative II

> *Est-ce que tu es au cinéma ?*
> Is it that you are in the cinema ?

After the expression "*Est-ce que*", if the next word starts with a vowel, then the expression becomes "*Est-ce qu'*"

> He is eating.
> *Il mange.*

Forme interrogative

> *Est-ce qu'il mange ?*
> Is it that he is eating ?

(c) Invert the subject and the verb and use a hyphen between them, and add a question mark at the end.

> You are watching the television.
> *Vous regardez la télévision.*

Forme interrogative III

> *Regardez-vous la télévision ?*
> Are you watching the television ?

After the inversion, if the verb ends with a vowel and the subject begins with a vowel, then add "-t-" between them, i.e. the letter t with 2 hyphens. This facilitates the pronunciation.

> He eats chicken.
> *Il manage du poulet.*

Forme interrogative III

> *Mange-t-il du poulet ?*
> Does he eat chicken ?

If the subject is not a pronoun, but a noun, then we begin the question with a noun, use a comma, then invert the verb and the relevant subject pronoun.

> The car is black
> *La voiture est noire.*

From interrogative III

> *La voiture, est-elle noire ?*
> Is the car black ?

Questions possible in French :

How many?	*Combien de ?*
How ?	*Comment ?*
When ?	*Quand ?*
Which ?	*Quel (m) ?*
	Quelle (f) ?
	Quels (m, pl) ?
	Quelles (f, pl) ?
Which one ?	*Lequel (m) ?*
	Laquelle (f) ?
	Lesquels (m, pl) ?
	Lesquelles (f, pl) ?
Where ?	*Où ?*
From where ?	*D'où ?*
Since when ?	*Depuis quand ?*
Why ?	*Pourquoi ?*
Of which colour ?	*De quelle couleur ?*
What is the time ?	*Quelle heure est-il ?*
At what time ?	*À quelle heure ?*
How is the wheather ?	*Quel temps fait-il ?*

What is this ?	*Qu'est-ce que c'est ?*
Is it that ?	*Est ce que…?*
What ?	*Que ?*
Who ?	*Qui ?*
To whom ?	*À qui*
About what ?	*De quoi ?*
Whose ?	*De qui ?*

25

SPORTS AND MUSICAL INSTRUMENTS
SPORTS ET INSTRUMENTS

SPORTS
LES SPORTS

Vocabulary

Hockey	*le hockey*
Cricket	*le cricket*
Football	*le football*
Basketball	*le basket*
Volleyball	*le volley*
Tennis	*le tennis*
Table-Tennis	*le ping-pong*
Badminton	*le badminton*
Baseball	*le base-ball*
Handball	*le hand-ball*
Swimming	*la natation*
Backstroke	*le dos crawlé*
Butterfly stroke	*la brasse papillon*
Freestyle	*la nage libre*
Breast stroke	*la brasse*

Gymnastics	*la gymnastique*
Relay	*la course de relais*
Marathon	*le marathon*
Sprint	*le sprint*
Hurdles	*les haies*
Track and field	*l'athlétisme*
Martial arts	*l'art martial*
Water-skiing	*le ski nautique*
Skiing	*le ski*
Downhill skiing	*le ski de piste*
Ice skating	*le partinage*
Roller skating	*le patin à roulettes*
Rugby	*le rugby*
Skating	*le partinage*
Discus	*le discus*
Javelin Throw	*le jet de javelot*
Shotput	*le shotput*
High Jump	*le saut élevé*
Long Jump	*le long saut*
Fencing	*l'escrime*
Wrestling	*la lutte*
Water Polo	*le water-polo*

Polo	*le polo*
Golf	*le golf*
Windsurfing	*la planche à voile*
Shooting	*le tournage*
Stand	*le nombre de points*
Court	*le court*
Stadium	*le stade*
Snooker	*le jeu de billard*
Billiards	*le jeu de billard*
Indoor games	*les sports pratiqués en salle*
Match	*le match*
Team	*l'équipe*
Referee	*l'arbitre*
Score	*le score*
Olympics	*les jeux olympiques*
Asian Games	*le jeux asiatiques*
Championship	*le championnat*
League	*la division*
Quater-final	*le quart de finale*
Semi-final	*la demi-finale*
Final	*la finale*
Runners up	*Second (e)*

To win	*réussir*
To lose	*échouer*
To participate	*participer*
Athletics	*l' athlétisme*
Cycling	*le cyclisme*
Horse-riding	*l' équitation*
Sailing	*la voile*
Fishing	*la pêche*
Biking	*le cyclisme*
Chess	*les échecs*
Cooking	*la cuisine*
Dancing	*la danse*
Gardening	*le jardinage*
Hiking	*la randonnée*
Hunting	*la chasse*
Jogging	*le jogging*
Archery	*le tir à l' arc*
Boxing	*la boxe*
Diving	*la plongée*
Board games	*les jeux de société*
Computer games	*les jeux vidéo*

MUSICAL INSTRUMENTS
LES INSTRUMENTS

Violin	*le violon*
Guitar	*la guitare*
Piano	*le piano*
Flute	*la flûte*
Xylophone	*le xylophone*
Mouth organ	*le harmonica*
Bagpipes	*la cornemuse*
Harmonium	*le harmonium*
Clarinet	*la clarinette*
Bugle	*le clairon*
Drum	*le tambour*
Bell	*la cloche*
Accordion	*l'accordéon*
Saxophone	*le saxophone*
Harp	*l'harpe*
Trumpet	*la trompette*
Windharp	*l'harpe éolienne*
Celtic / Irish harp	*l'harpe celtique / irlandaise*

Dialogue

Marc : Are you a sportsman (sportswoman) ?
Est-ce que vous êtes sportif (sportive) ?

Diego : Yes I am a sportsman.
Oui je suis sportif.

Marc : Do you like sports ?
Est-ce que vous aimez le sport ?

Diego : Yes, I love sports.
Oui, j'adore le sport.

Marc : What do you play as sports ?
Qu'est-ce que vous faites, comme sports ?

Diego : I play tennis and I swim.
Je joue au tennis et je fais de la natation.

Marc : Do you play a musical instrument ?
Est-ce que vous jouez d'un instrument de musique ?

Diego : No, I don't play any instrument.
Non, je ne joue pas d'instrument.

With instruments, the verb 'Jouer' is used. The instrument is preceded by the articles *Du, De la, De l'* or *Des,* depending on the gender, number and the beginning letter of the instrument.

I play piano.
Je joue du piano.

I play violin.
Je joue du violon.

I play guitar.
Je joue de la guitare..

I play accordion.
Je joue de l'accordéon.

I play drums.
Je joue des tambours.

With sports, the verb *'faire'* and *'jouer'* are used. With the verb *'jouer'*, the game is preceded by the articles *Au, À la, À l'* or *Aux,* depending on the gender, number and the beginning letter of the game.

I play cricket.
Je joue au cricket.

I play chess.
Je joue aux échecs.

With the verb 'faire', the game is preceded by the articles *Du, De la, De l'* or *Des,* depending on the gender, number and the beginning letter of the game.

I ski.
Je fais du ski.

I wrestle.
Je fais de la lutte.

I do martial arts.
Je fais de l' art martial.

I play board games.
Je joue des jeux de société.

26

NEGATIVE FORM
FORME NÉGATIVE

In French, to change a simple sentence into negative form, "*ne*" and "*pas*" are added before and after the conjugated verb.

> I eat.
> *Je mange.*

> I don't eat.
> *Je ne mange pas.*

"*Ne*" changes to "*N*" before the vowels A, E, I, O, U and H.

> He is tall.
> *Il est grand.*

> He is not tall.
> *Il n'est pas grand.*

> She lives in Paris.
> *Elle habite à Paris.*

> She doesn't live in Paris.
> *Elle n'habite pas à Paris.*

Sometimes NE is omitted in the oral form.

> I don't know.
> *Je sais pas.*   *instead of.*
> *Je ne sais pas.*

There are other negative forms in French.

ne... plus (no longer)

I no longer eat tomatoes.
*Je **ne** mange **plus** les tomates.*

ne... jamais (never)

I never eat tomatoes.
*Je **ne** mange **jamais** les tomates.*

ne... rien (nothing)

Diego ate nothing.
*Diego **n' a rien** mangé.*

ne... personne (nobody)

I want to see nobody.
*Je ne veux voir **personne**.*

ne... pas encore (not yet)

I have not yet finished the work.
*Je n' ai **pas encore** fini le trovail.*

ne... pas du tout (not at all)

I am not at all thirsty.
*Je n' ai **pas du tout** soif.*

ne... aucun(e) (none)

I have no idea.
*Je n' ai **aucune** idée.*

ne... que (only)

He is only 5 years old.
Il n' a que cinq ans.

ne... ni... ni (neither ... nor)

I neither eat ham nor chicken.
Je ne mange ni jambon ni poulet.

ne... guère (hardly)

I hardly speak to Shiv.
Je ne parle guère à Shiv.

Personne and *Rien* can be used at the beginning of a sentence as subject pronouns, followed by *Ne* or *N'*.

Nobody likes studying.
Personne n'aime étudier.

Nothing is available.
Rien n'est disponible.

27

THE MEALS
LES REPAS

Vocabulary

Breakfast	*Le petit déjeuner*
Lunch	*Le déjeuner*
Snacks	*Le goûter*
Dinner	*Le dîner*
Boire	To drink
Manger	To eat
Prendre	To take

Boire (To drink)

Je bois

Tu bois

Il boit

Elle boit

Nous buvons

Vous buvez

Ils boivent

Elles biovent

Manger (To eat)

Je mange

Tu manges

Il mange

Elle mange

Nous mangeons

Vous mangez

Ils mangent

Elles mangent

Prendre (To take)

Je prends

Tu prends

Il prend

Elle prend

Nous prenons

Vous prenez

Ils prennent

Elles prennent

Examples :

I have my breakfast
Je prends mon petit déjeuner.

I have my lunch
Je prends mon déjeuner.
Je déjeune.

I have my snacks
Je prends mon goûter.
Je goûte.

I have my dinner
Je prends mon dîner.
Je dîne.

Starter	*un hors d'œuvre.*
main course	*le plat principal*
sweet/dessert	*le dessert*

Quantity

a box of	*une boîte de*
a tin of	*une boîte de*
a bottle of	*une bouteille de*
a litre of	*un litre de*
a piece of	*un morceau de*
a packet of	*un paquet de*
a portion of	*une portion de*
a slice of	*une tranche de*
a pound of	*une livre de*
a kilo of	*un kilo de*
half a kilo of	*un demi-kilo de*
10 grams of	*10 grammes de*

Shops

butcher's	*la boucherie*
baker's	*la boulangerie*
grocer's	*l'épicerie*
cake shop	*la pâtisserie*
pork butcher's	*la charcuterie*
tobacconist's	*le bureau de tabac*
dairy	*le crémier*
fish market	*le poissonnier*

28

PARTITIVE ARTICLES
ARTICLES PARTITIFS

The partitive articles indicate an indefinite quantity of something, usually food or drink. It can be translated as some, or any in English, or can even be omitted. There are four partitive articles used, depending on the number, gender and the first letter used.

DU	masculine singular
DE LA	feminine singular
DE L'	vowel
DES	plural

The partitive articles are used for food and drinks because we usually consume a part of it. But if we consume the whole thing, we use the definite article

I eat some bread
Je mange du pain.

I eat the (whole) bread.
Je mange le pain.

The partitive articles are used for an unknown and an uncountable quantity. When the quantity is known or countable, we use the indefinite article.

I ate some tart.
J'ai mangé de la tarte.

I prepared a tart.
J'ai préparé une tarte.

All the four forms of partitive articles (*Du, De la, De l', Des*) change to *De* in the negative form, or *D'* if the noun starts with a vowel.

I eat cake.
Je mange du gâteau.

I don't eat cake.
Je ne mange pas de gâteau.

I drink water.
Je bois de l' eau.

I don't drink water.
Je ne bois pas d' eau.

THINGS TO EAT
LES CHOSES À MANGER

butter	*du beurre*
biscuit	*de la biscotte*
carrot	*de la carotte*
jam	*de la confiture*
croissant	*du croissant*
chips	*des frites*
cheese	*du fromage*
honey	*du miel*

bread	*du pain*
peas	*des petits pois*
pizza	*de la pizza*
fish	*du poisson*
soup	*du potage*
salad	*de la viande*
vegetables	*des légumes*
cabbage	*du chou*
cauliflower	*du chou-fleur*
French beans	*des haricots verts*
potato	*de la pomme de terre*
sweets	*des bonbons*
an ice-cream	*une glace*
a hot dog	*un hot-dog*
ham	*du jambon*
onion	*du ognion*
pork	*du porc*
chicken	*du poulet*
beef	*du rosbif*
steak	*du steak*
a lollipop	*une sucette*

sandwiches	*des sandwichs*
tomato	*de la tomate*
mushrooms	*des champignons*
flour	*de la farine*
calf	*du veau*
lamb	*de l'agneau*
mustard	*de la moutarde*
rabbit	*du lapin*
beef	*du boeuf*
omelet	*de l'omelette*
yogurt	*de la yaourt*
salt	*du sel*
pepper	*du poivre*
oil	*de l' huile*
vinegar	*du vinaigre*
cake	*du gâteau*
quiche	*une quiche*
pie/pâté	*du pâté*
pancake	*de la crêpe*
sausage	*de la saucisse*
chocolate mousse	*de la mousse au chocolat*

caramel cream	*de la crème caramel*
cock	*du coq*
spinach	*du épinard*
radish	*du radis*
turnip	*du navet*
garlic	*de l'ail*
garlic bread	*du pain à l'ail*
ginger	*du gingembre*
parsley	*du persil*
sauce	*de la sauce*
coriander	*de la coriandre*
mint	*de la menthe*
cucumber	*du concombre*
jackfruit	*du jaque*
duck	*du canard*
French stick (bread)	*de la baguette*
lolly	*du bâtonnet*
waffle	*de la gaufre*
hamburger	*du hamburger*
pasta	*des pâtes*
eggs	*des œufs*
salami	*du saucisson*

FRUIT
DES FRUITS

banana	*une banane*
strawberry	*une fraise*
melon	*un melon*
orange	*une orange*
peach	*une pêche*
pear	*une poire*
apple	*une pomme*
grapes	*du raisin*
walnut	*de la noix*
cashewnut	*de la noix de cajou*
date	*de la datte*
pistachio	*de la pistache*
almond	*de l'amande*
coconut	*de la noix de coco*
apricot	*de l'abricot*
cherry	*de la cerise*
mango	*de la mangue*
muskmelon	*du cantaloup*
sugarcane	*une canne à sucre*

pineapple	*un ananas*
lychee	*un litchi*
pomegranate	*une grenade*
guava	*une goyave*
papaya	*une papaye*
plum	*une prune*

BEVERAGES
DES BOISSONS

hot drinks	*des boissons chaudes*
cold drinks	*des boissons froides*
coffee	*du café*
white coffee	*du café-crème*
hot chocolate	*du chocolat*
tea	*du thé*
lemon tea	*du thé au citron*
water	*de l'eau*
mineral water	*de l'eau minérale*
fruit juice	*du jus de fruit*
milk	*du lait*
lemonade	*de la limonade*

wine	*du vin*
champagne	*de la champagne*
orange juice	*de l'orangeade*
fruit syrup	*du sirop*
soft drinks	*de la boisson non alcoolisées*
green tea	*du thé vert*
jasmine tea	*du thé au jasmin*
soda water	*de l'eau de settz*
whisky	*du whisky*
tomato juice	*du jus de tomate*
pineapple juice	*du jus d'ananas*
apple brandy	*de l'eau de vie de pommes*
brandy	*du cognac*
cognac	*du cognac*
gin	*du gin*
ginger beer	*de la boisson gazeuse au gingembre*
vodka	*de la vodka*
cocktail	*du cocktail*
martini	*du martini*
sherry	*du xérès*
beer	*de la bière*

SPICES
LES ÉPICES

salt	*le sel*
pepper	*le poivre*
red chilly	*le poivron rouge*
turmeric	*le curcuma*
	le safron des Indes
ginger	*le gingembre*
garlic	*l'ail*
cinnamon	*la cannelle*
cardamon	*la cardamome*
cumin	*le cumin*
cloves	*le clou de girofle*
saffron	*le safran*
nutmeg	*la muscade*
aniseed	*la graine d'anis*
green pepper	*le poivron vert*

29

AT THE RESTAURANT
AU RESTAURANT

Vocabulary

cutlery	*les couverts*
spoon	*la cuiller*
fork	*la fourchette*
knife	*le couteau*
napkin	*la serviette*
table cloth	*la nappe*
to order	*demander*
tip	*la pourboire*
menu	*le menu*
bill	*l'addition*
waiter	*le garçon*
to lay the table	*metre la couverte*
plate	*l'assiette*
bowl	*le bol*
dish	*le plat*
casserole	*le casserole*

bottle	*la bouteille*
glass	*le verre*
cup	*la tasse*
toothpick	*le cure-dent*
fresh food	*la nourriture-fraîche*
tinned food	*les conserves*
to be hungry	*avoir faim*
to be thirsty	*avoir soif*
reservation	*la réservation*
to serve	*servir*
French cuisine	*la cuisine française*
Indian cuisine	*la cuisine indienne*
expensive	*cher*
delicious	*délicieux*
sumptuous	*somptueux*
helping	*la portion*
taste	*le goût*
tablespoon	*la cuiller de service*
teaspoon	*la petite cuiller*

Dialogue

A : Diego, let's eat in a restaurant today !
Diego, mangeons dans un restaurant aujourd' hui

B : In which restaurant ? You want to eat French food or Indian food ?
Dans quel restaurant ? Voulez-vous manger la cuisine française ou la cuisine indienne ?

A : I prefer the French cuisine.
Je préfère la cuisine française.

C : Welcome Sir
Bienvenu monsieur.

B : A table for 2 please.
Une table pour 2 personnes, s'il vous plaît.

C : Have you reserved a table ?
Avez-vous reservé une table ?

B : Yes
Oui

C : Under which name ?
Sous quel nom ?

B : Mr. Vincent
M. Vincent

C : The restaurant is full today.
Le restaurant est plein aujourd' hui.

B : Yes there are many people.
Oui, il y a beaucoup de monde.

C : What would you like to eat for starters ?
Qu'est-ce que vous voulez pour l'entrée.

B : Some cheese please
Du fromage s'il vous plaît.

C : Would you want something to drink ?
Voulez-vous boire quelque chose ?

B : 1 juice and 1 coffee.
Un jus et un café.

C : Can I take the order.
Voulez-vous demander ?

B : After a few minutes.
Après quelques minutes.

C : What do you want to eat sir ?
Qu'est-ce que vous voulez manger monsieur ?

B : Snails, a bowl of rice and chicken.
Des escargots, un bol du riz et du poulet.

C : Anything else ?
Quelquechose d'autre ?

B : Salad and yogurt.
De la salade et du yaourt.

C : Is that all ?
C'est tout ?

B : Yes, for the moment.
Oui, pour le moment.

C : What do you want for dessert ?
Qu'est-ce que vous prendrez pour le dessert ?

B : I want some chocolate cake. And you ?
Je veux du gâteau au chocolat. Et toi ?

A : I prefer some fresh fruits.
Je préfère des fruits frais.

C : Have a good meal.
Bon appetit.

B : Please hurry.
Vite, s'il vous plaît.

C : Is that all for the day ?
C'est tout pour le jour ?

B : Yes, the meal was delicious.
Oui, le repas était délicieux.

A : Bill please.
L'addition, s'il vous plaît.

C : Here you are, sir.
Voilà monsieur.

A : Give him a good tip.
Donne-lui un bon pourboire.

C : Thank you very much.
Merci beaucoup.

B : Goodbye !
Au revoir.

C : See you soon !
À bientôt.

30

AT THE POST OFFICE
À LA POSTE

Vocabulary

postage stamp	*le timbre*
post card	*la carte postale*
letter	*la lettre*
card	*la carte*
parcel	*le paquet*
envelope	*l'envelope*
money order	*le mandat-poste*
telegram	*le télégramme*
postcode	*le code postal*
address	*l'adresse*
STD	*l'automatique*
ISDN	*RNIS*
mailbox	*la boîte aux lettres*
postbox	*la boîte aux lettres*
postage	*les tarifs postaux*
mailbag	*le sac postal*
by mail	*par la poste*

mail car	*le wagon postal*
postman	*le facteur*
STD code	*l'indicatif de zone*
airmail	*la post aérienne*
by airmail	*par avion*

DIALOGUE

A : Where is the post office ?
Où est la poste ?

B : The post office is on the left.
La poste est à gauche.

A : At what time does the post office open ?
À quelle heure la poste ouvre-t-elle ?

B : The post office opens at 10.00 am.
La poste ouvre à 10 heures.

A : At what time does the post office close ?
À quelle heure la poste ferme-t-elle ?

B : The post office closes at 5 p.m.
La poste ferme à 17 heures.

A : I want to send a parcel.
Je veux envoyer un paquet.

B : By mail or by airmail ?
Par la poste ou par avion ?

A : I want to send this letter by post and this parcel by airmail.

Je veux envoyer cette lettre par la poste et ce paquet par avion.

B : How much does it cost to mail a letter in France ?

Ça coûte combien pour envoyer une lettre en France?

A : It costs 10 euros.

Ça coûte 10 euros.

A : What is the postage for a letter to India ?

Quel est le tarif postal pour une lettre en Inde ?

B : It is 15 euros.

Ça coûte 15 euros.

A : In how many days will it reach ?

Elle arrivera dans combien de jours ?

B : It will reach in 7 days.

Elle arrivera dans 7 jours.

A : Where must I put the letter ?

Où est-ce qu'il faut mettre la lettre ?

B : Put it in the mail box.

Mettez-la dans la boîte aux lettres ?

A : Please give me some postage stamps.

Donnez-moi des timbres s'il vous plaît.

B : Here it is 50 euros please.

Voilà, 50 euros s'il vous plaît.

A : Where is the head office ?
Où est le bureau de poste principal ?

B : It is behind the post office.
Il est derrière la poste.

A : I need 2 postcards please.
J'ai besoin de 2 cartes postales, s'il vous plaît.

B : Please check the mailing address.
Vérifiez l'adresse postale s'il vous plaît.

A : What is the post code for India ?
Quel est le code postal de l' Inde ?

B : It is 11.
C'est 11.

A : I wish to send a money-order to India.
Je veux envoyer un mandat-poste en Inde.

B : For how many euros ?
De combien d'euros ?

A : Only 500 euros
Seulement 500 euros.

B : What is the STD code of Paris ?
Quel est l'indicatif de zone de Paris ?

31

SHOPPING
LES COURSES

A : I want to go for shopping. Where is the market ?
Je voudrais faire du shopping. Où est le marché ?

B : What do you want to buy ?
Qu'est-ce que vous voulez acheter ?

A : I want to buy clothes and fruits.
Je voudrais acheter des vêtements et des fruits.

B : To buy clothes you can go to the market Rock and to buy fruits, go to the fruit market.
Pour acheter des vêtements, vous pouvez aller au marché Rock et pour acheter des fruits, allez au marché des fruits.

A : Thank you very much.
Merci beaucoup.

C : Good morning ma'am, what do you want ?
Bonjour madame, désirez ?

A : Good morning. I want to buy a shirt.
Bonjour. Je voudrais acheter une chemise.

C : Of which colour ?
De quelle couleur ?

A : I prefer blue.
Je préfère bleu.

C : Light blue or dark blue ?
Bleu chair ou bleu foncé ?

A : Show me both.
Montrez-moi les deux.

C : Here you are. But of what size ?
Voilà. Mais de quelle taille.

A : A large.
Un 'large'.

C : A cotton or a silk shirt ?
Une chemise en coton ou en soie ?

A : A cotton shirt. My husband doesn't like wearing silk shirts.
Une chemise en coton. Mon mari n'aime pas porter les chemises en soie.

C : Anything else ma'am ?
Quelquechose d'autre, madame ?

A : Yes, I also want a skirt and a tie.
Oui, je voudrais aussi acheter une jupe et une cravate.

C : The ties are on the first floor and the skirts on the second.
Les cravates sont au premier étage. et les jupes au deuxième.

A : I want to buy this tie.
Je voudrais acheter cette cravate.

C : Sure ma'am.
Biensûr, madame.

A : How much is it for ?
Ça coûte combien ?

C : It cost 20 euros.
Ça coûte 20 euros.

A : But this is very expensive, I will see another one.
Mais c'est trop cher, Je verrai un autre.

C : Do you like this tie ?
Aimez-vous cette cravate ?

A : Yes, this one is better, how much is it for ?
Oui, celle-ci est meilleure, ça coûte combien ?

C : Only 12 euros.
Seulement 12 euros.

A : OK. I will buy it. Where are the skirts ?
D'accord. Je vais l'acheter. Où sont les jupes ?

C : Second floor.
Au deuxième étage.

A : Can you please show me some silk skirts ?
Pourriez-vous me montrer quelques jupes de soie s'il vous plaît ?

C : Which colour do you prefer ?
De quelle couleur préférez vous ?

A : A red skirt.
Une jupe rouge.

C : Sorry, it's not available at the moment.
Désolée, elle n'est pas disponible à ce moment.

A : Where should I pay for the shirt and the tie ?
Où est-ce qu'il faut payer pour la chemise et la cravate ?

C : At the cash counter.
Au caissier.

A : How much does that make ?
Ça fait combien ?

A : How much do the apples cost ?
Combien coûtent les pommes ?

C : The apples cost 10 euros a kg.
Les pommes coûtent 10 euros par kilogramme.

A : You are asking for a lot.
Vous demandez beaucoup.

C : The prices are fixed ma'am
Les prix sont fixes, madame.

A : Give me half a kilo apples.
Donnez-moi un demi-kilo de pommes.

C : Anything else ?
Quelquechose d'autres ?

A : How much are the grapes for ?
Combien coûtent les raisins ?

C : 10 euros a kg.
10 euros par kilo.

A : Are they fresh ?
Sont-ils-frais ?

C : Yes ma'am.
Oui madame.

A : OK, then give me 2 kgs of raisins.
D'accord, donnez-moi 2 kilos de raisins.

C : Is that all ?
C'est tout ?

A : Yes, that makes it how much ?
Oui, Ça fait combien ?

C : 25 euros. Will you pay by cheque ?
Payez-vous par chèque ?

A : Do you accept credit cards ?
Acceptez-vous les cartes de crédit ?

C : Yes ma'am.
Oui madame.

A : Ah, that's good.
Ah, c'est bon.

vocabulary

A kilogram	*un kilogramme*
A gram	*un gramme*
A milligram	*un milligramme*
A litre	*un litre*
A kilometer	*un kilomètre*
A meter	*un mètre*
A centimeter	*un centimètre*
A decimeter	*un décimètre*
A pound	*une livre*
Half a kilo	*un demi-kilo*

32

AT THE AIRPORT
À L' AÉROPORT

Vocabulary

A ticket	*un billet*
economy	*économique*
1st class	*1re classe*
reservation	*une réservation*
destination	*la destination*
to book the luggage	*l'enregistrement des bagages*
to pass at the customs	*passer à la douane*
a custom officer	*un douanier*
to check the luggage	*fouillir les bagages*
to declare	*déclarer*
to pay custom duty	*payer les droits de douane*
to present the identification papers	*présenter les papiers d'identité*
a passport	*un passeport*
a visa	*un visa*
an identity card	*une carte d'identité*
to fill a form	*remplir une fiche*

a form	*un formulaire*
luggage	*des bagages*
passport control	*le contrôle des passeports*
the terminal	*le hall*
a passenger	*un voyageur*
an immigration officer	*un policier*

Dialogue

A : How long will you stay here ?
Vous allez rester ici pour combien de jours ?

B : What is the purpose of your visit ?
Quelle est la raison de votre visite ?

A : I am here for holidays.
Je suis ici en vacances.

B : Your passport please.
Votre passeport, s'il vous plaît.

A : Here is my passport.
Voilà mon passeport.

B : Do you have anything to declare ?
Est-ce que vous avez quelque chose à déclarer ?

A : Yes a small bottle of perfume and half a litre of Canadian whisky.
Oui, un petit flacon de parfum et un demi-litre de whisky canadien.

B : Do you have any luggage ?
Est-ce que vous avez des bagages ?

A : Yes, a big bag.
Oui un grand sac.

B : Please show your papers.
Montrez vos papiers, s'il vous plaît.

A : Here they are.
Voilà.

B : And your visa also.
Et aussi votre visa.

A : You will have to pay custom duty.
Il faut payer les droits de douane.

B : Please fill the form.
Remplissez le formulaire s'il vous plaît.

A : I have a camera for personal use, will I have to pay a duty on this ?
J'ai un appareil de photo pour mon usage personel, est-ce qu'il faut payer les droits de douane pour ça?

33

AT THE STATION
À LA GARE

Vocabulary

ticket	*le billet*
ticket machine	*la batterie automatique*
buffet	*le buffet*
information office	*le bureau de renseignements*
corner	*le coin*
to stamp your ticket	*composter votre billet*
left luggage	*la consigne*
corridor	*le couloir*
time table	*l'horaire*
smoking	*fumeur*
non-smoking	*non-fumeur*
ticket office	*le guichet*
kiosk	*le kiosque*
platform	*le quai*
reserved seat	*la réservation*
waiting room	*la salle d'attente*
platform/track	*la voie*

train carriage	*la voiture*
dining car	*le wagon-restaurant*
bagage van	*le fourgon*
platform ticket	*le billet de quai*
first class	*la première classe*
second class	*la deuxième classe*
window seat	*le coin fenêtre*
isle	*le coin couloir*
one-way	*aller simple*
two-way	*aller retour*
departure	*le départ*
arrival	*l'arrivé*
entry	*l'entrée*
exit	*la sortie*

Dialogue

A : The train for Strasbourg leaves at what time ?
Le train pour Strasbourg part à quelle heure ?

B : At 10:15.
À 10h 15.

A : And it arrives at what time ?
Et il arrive à quelle heure ?

B : At 2:30.
À 14h 30.

A : Is it a direct train ?
C'est direct ?

B : No, you must change at Politiers.
Non, il faut changer à Politiers.

A : The train leaves from which platform ?
Le train part de quel quai ?

B : It leaves from platform 2.
Il part de quai numéro 2.

A : A ticket for Strasbourg, please.
Un billet pour Strasbourg, s'il vous plaît.

B : One-way or return ?
Aller simple ou aller-retour ?

A : One-way.
Aller simple.

B : First class or second class ?
Première classe ou deuxième classe ?

A : First class.
 : *Première class.*

B : You want 'smoking' or 'non-smoking'.
Vous voulez 'fumeurs' ou 'non-fumeurs' ?

A : Non smoking.
Non-fumeurs.

B : Do you want a corner seat or isle ?
Vous voulez coin fenître ou coin couloir ?

A : I want the window seat.
Je voudrais le coin-fenêtre.

B : Here, your seat number is 11.
Voilà, votre place est le numéro 11.

A : Thank you very much, sir.
Merci beaucoup Monsieur.

B : Here is your ticket and your reservation, 300 euros.
Voilà votre billet et votre réservation, 300 euros s'il vous plaît.

A : Thank you, where is the waiting room ?
Merci, où est la salle d'attente ?

B : On the left.
À gauche.

34

AT THE DOCTOR'S
CHEZ LE MÉDECIN

Vocabulary

allergy	*l'allergie*
antibiotic	*l'antibiotique*
AIDS	*SIDA*
arthritis	*l'arthrite*
appendicitis	*l'appendicite*
abdominal laparotomy	*l'aparotomie abdominal*
ambulance	*l'ambulance*
anesthesia	*l'anesthésie*
antibacterial	*antibactérien*
abortion	*l'avortement*
acidity	*l'acidité*
asthma	*l'asthme*
blood test	*l'analyse de sang*
bandage	*la bande*
blood transfusion	*la transfusion sanguine*
blood bank	*la banque du sang*
blood group	*le group sanguin*

backache	*le mal de dos*
burn	*la brûlure*
bronchitis	*la bronchite*
brain tumour	*la tumeur au cerveau*
balm	*le baume*
cancer	*le cancer*
chicken pox	*la varicelle*
chronic	*chronique*
contagious	*contagieux*
cardiovascular	*cardio-vasculaire*
coronary heart disease	*la maladie coronarienne*
CAT Scan	*la scanographie*
cramp	*la crampe*
diabetes	*le diabète*
dandruff	*les pellicules*
dentist	*le/la dentiste*
ear infection	*l'otite*
emergency	*le service des urgences*
E.N.T.	*ORL*
ECG	*L'ECG*
EEG	*L'EEG*
electrotherapy	*l'électrothérapie*

epidemic	*l'épidémie*
eardrops	*les gouttes pour les oreilles*
eye drops	*les gouttes pour les yeux*
fracture	*la fracture*
gastroenteritis	*la gastroentérite*
glucose	*le glucose*
gynaecologist	*le/la gynécologue*
gall-stone	*le calcul bilaire*
heart rate	*le rythme cardiaque*
heart disease	*la maladie de coeur*
heart attack	*la crise cardiaque*
hyper tension	*la hypertension*
heart transplant	*la greffe du coeur*
infection	*l'infection*
intravenous injection	*la pîqure intraveineuse*
intramuscular injection	*la pîqure intramusculaire*
intravenous drip	*la perfusion intraveineuse*
insect bite	*la pîqure d'insectes*
jaundice	*la jaunice*
kidney-stone	*le calcul-rénal*
mixture	*la préparation*
malaria	*la malaria*

measles	*la rougeole*
miscarriage	*la fausse-couche*
massage	*le massage*
nurse	*l'infirmier*
nutrition	*la nutrition*
ointment	*l'onguent*
osteoporosis	*l'ostéoporose*
osteoarthritis	*l'ostéoarthrite*
paediatrician	*le/la pédiatre*
paediatrics	*la pédiatrie*
pneumonia	*la pneumonie*
physiotherapy	*la physiothérapie*
painkiller	*le calmant*
polio	*la polio*
powder	*la poudre*
rheumatoid arthritis	*la polyarthrite*
rheumatology	*la rhumatologie*
rheumatism	*le rhumatisme*
sleeping pill	*le somnifère*
small-pox	*la petite vérole*
sterilisation	*la stérilisation*
surgery	*la chirurgie*

surgeon	*le chirurgien*
swelling	*la grosseur*
sun-stroke	*l'insolation*
skin disease	*la maladie de peau*
thermometer	*le thermomètre*
tuberculosis	*la tuberculose*
tablet	*le comprimé*
tetanus	*le tétanos*
ulcer	*l'ulcère*
ultra-sound	*l'ultrasons*
virus	*le virus*
venereal disease	*la maladie vénérienne*
vitamin	*la vitamine*
wheelchair	*le fauteuil roulant*
xenophobia	*la xénophobie*
xenophobic	*le xénophobe*
X-ray	*les rayons-x*
To be in good health	*Être en bonne santé*
To be ill	*Être malade*
To have a headache	*Avoir mal à la tête*
To have a toothache	*Avoir mal aux dents*

To have an arm ache	*Avoir mal au bras*
To have fever	*Avoir de la fièvre*
To have a stomach-ache	*Avoir mal au ventre*
To have throat pain	*Avoir mal à la gorge*
To have pain in the eyes	*Avoir mal aux yeux*
To have pain in the ears	*Avoir mal aux oreilles*
To have pain in the hand	*Avoir mal à la main*
To have pain in the leg	*Avoir mal à la jambe*
To have a backache	*Avoir mal au dos*
To have a cold	*Être enrhûmé*
To cure	*soigner*
To recover	*guérir*
soap	*un savon*
sunscreen lotion	*une crème solaire*
cotton	*un coton*
shampoo	*du shampooing*
asprin	*l'aspirine*
toothpaste	*un tube de dentifrice*
toothbrush	*une brosse à dents*
syrup	*du sirop*
medicine	*un médicament*

injection	*une piqûre*
bandage	*une bande*
lozenge	*une pastille*
Band-Aid	*sparadrap*
prescription	*une ordonnance*
appointment	*un rendez-vous*
patient	*un malade*

Dialogue

Doctor : How are you ?
Médecin: Comment allez-vous ?

Patient : I have a headache.
Malade : J'ai mal à la tête.

Doctor : You no more feel tired ?
Médecin: Vous n'êtes plus fatiqué ?

Patient : No, but I don't sleep well.
Malade : Non, mais je ne dors pas bien.

Doctor : Ok, I'll give you medicines for your sleep and headache.
Médecin: Bon, je vais vous donner des médicaments pour dormir et pour le mal à la tête.

Patient : Doctor, I also have pain in the eyes.
Malade : Docteur, j'ai aussi mal aux yeux.

Doctor : Lie down, I'll put eye drops.
Médecin : *Couchez-vous, je vais mettre des gouttes des yeux.*

Patient : Thank you doctor. How much ?
Malade : *Merci, docteur. Ça fait combien ?*

Doctor : 100 euros and here is the prescription.
Médecin : *100 euros. et voilà l'ordonnance.*

35

AT THE BANK
À LA BANQUE

Vocabulary

bank account	*un compte bancaire*
bank balance	*un solde bancaire*
bank book	*un carnet de banque*
bank card	*une carte d'identité bancaire*
Reserve Bank	*une banque de réserve*
bank note	*un billet*
exchange bureau	*un bureau de change*
credit card	*une carte de credit*
exchange rate	*le cours de change*
a currency	*une devise*
coin	*une pièce*
change	*la monnaie*
traveller's cheque	*un cheque de voyage*
money	*l'argent*
cash counter	*la caisse*
bank manager	*un directeur d'agence*
cashier	*un caissier*

account number	*le numéro de compte*
cheque book	*un carnet de chèques*
cheque account	*un compte chèque*
ATM	*GAB*
withdrawl slip	*un bordereau de retrait*
deposit slip	*un bulletin de versement*
bond	*un bon*
loan	*un crédit*
bank draft	*une traite bancaire*
U.S. Dollar	*un dollar américain*
bank rate	*le taux d'escompte*
Euro	*l'euro*
Canadian Dollar	*un dollar canadien*
fixed deposit	*le dépôt fixe*
(German) Mark	*le mark*
(Indian) Rupee	*la roupie*
Pound	*une livre*
deposit bank	*la banque de dépôt*
(Japanese) Yen	*le yen*
bank transfer	*le virement bancaire*
Rouble	*le rouble*
bank charges	*les frais bancaires*

Dialogue

A : Where must I go to change the money ?
Où est-ce qu'il faut aller pour changer de l'argent s'il vous plaît ?

B : Go down there, miss – at the 'Exchange counter'
Allez là-bas, Mademoiselle – au 'change'.

A : Good morning sir, I want to change a traveller's cheque, please.
Bonjour Monsieur, Je voudrais changer un chèque de voyage s'il vous plaît.

C : Yes, ma'am do you have your passport ?
Oui Madame, vous avez votre passeport ?

A : Yes, here it is.
Oui, le voilà.

C : What is your address in France ?
Quelle est votre adresse en France ?

A : C/o Mr. & Mrs. Guile, Church Street, Saint Denis.
Chez M. et Mme Guile, rue de l'église, saint Denis.

C : Thank you, please sign here.
Merci, voulez – vous signer là, s'il vous plaît.

A : I want to change some money please.
Je voudrais changer de l'argent, s'il vous plaît.

C : Yes, sir, which currency ?
Oui Monsieur, C'est quelle devise ?

A : The Indian Rupee.
La roupie.

C : How many do you want to change ?
Vous voulez changer combien ?

A : 1000 rupees.
1000 roupies.

C : Thank you, wait at the cash counter please.
Merci, attendez à la caisse, s'il vous plaît.

A : I want to deposit 1000 rupees in the current account.
Je voudrais déposer 1000 roupies dans le compte.

C : Please fill in your name and amount in the deposit slip.
Écrivez votre nom et la somme sur le bulletin de versement.

A : What is the interest rate ?
Quelle est la taux d'intérêt ?

C : The interest rate is 5%.
C'est 5%.

A : Can I withdraw the fixed deposit in advance ?
Puis-je retirer le dépôt fixe en avance ?

C : Yes, you can.
Oui, vous pouvez.

A : Can I get a loan ?
Pouvez-vous m'accorder un prêt ?

C : You need to fill this form.
Il faut remplir cette fiche.

A : Can I meet the bank manager ?
Je voudrais rencontrer le directeur d'agence.

C : Sure sir, you must wait for a few minutes.
Biensûr Monsieur, il faut attendre quelques minutes.

36

SCHOOL
ÉCOLE

Vocabulary

to teach	*enseigner*
teaching	*l'enseignement*
to understand	*comprendre*
to learn	*apprendre*
a school boy	*un écolier*
a school girl	*une écolière*
montessori	*école maternelle*
primary school	*école primaire*
secondary school	*collège*
high school	*lycée*
university	*université*
library	*la bibliothèque*
playground	*la cour*
canteen	*la cantine*
a dayboarder	*un demi-pensionnaire*
gym	*le gymnase*
a boarding pupil	*un(e) interne*

boarding school	*un internat*
classroom	*la salle de classe*
school uniform	*un uniforme scolaire*
sports ground	*le terrain de sports*
laboratory	*un laboratoire*
book	*le livre*
notebook	*le cahier*
lesson	*la leçon*
chapter	*le chapitre*
timetable	*l'emploi du temps*
lunch break	*la pause-déjeuner*
break	*la récréation*
vacations	*les vacances*
subject	*la matière*
modern languages	*les langues vivantes*
German	*l'allemand*
English	*l'anglais*
French	*le français*
art and craft	*les arts plastiques*
art	*le dessin*
music	*la musique*
Spanish	*l'espagnol*

P.E. physical education	*l'éducation physique et sportive EPS*
religious education	*l'instruction réligieuse*
technology	*la technologie*
geography	*la géographie*
history	*l'histoire*
civics	*l'instruction civique*
mathematics	*les mathématiques*
economics	*l'économie*
natural sciences	*les sciences naturelles*
physics	*la physique*
biology	*la biologie*
chemistry	*la chimie*

Dialogue

A : How many students are there in your secondary school ?
Combien d'étudiants y a-t-il dans votre collège ?

B : There are about 700 students in our high school. It is a co-ed school.
Il y a environ 700 élèves dans notre lycée. C'est une école mixte.

A : At what time does the class start ?
À quelle heure commence le cours ?

B : The class starts at 8 o'clock.
Le cours commence à 8 heures.

A : What do you do in Physical Education ?
Qu'est ce que vous faites pour l'education physique et sportive ?

B : For PE we go to the gym and to the sports ground.
Pour EPS, nous allons dans le gymnase ou sur le terrain de sports.

A : Do you have a uniform ?
Avez vous un uniforme ?

B : Yes, we wear a school uniform.
Oui, nous portons un uniforme scolaire.

A. : At what time is the lunch break ?
La pause déjeuner est à quelle heure ?

B : It is at 11 o'clock and lasts for 15 minutes.
Elle est à 11 heures et elle dure 15 minutes.

A : What is your favourite subject ?
Quelle est votre matière préférée ?

B : I like maths and chemistry.
J'aime les mathématiques et la chimie.

A : How many holidays are there in France ?
Combien de vacances y a-t-il en France ?

B : In France there are about 16 weeks of vacations, in addition there are some holidays.
En France on a environ 16 semaines de vacances. En plus, il y a de petits congés.

37
PROFESSIONS
PROFESSIONS

Vocabulary	Masculine	Feminine
doctor	*médecin*	*médecin*
professor	*professeur*	*professeur*
teacher	*instituteur*	*institutrice*
dancer	*danseur*	*danseuse*
director	*directeur*	*directrice*
principal	*directeur*	*directrice*
singer	*chanteur*	*chanteuse*
actor	*acteur*	*actrice*
cook	*cuisinier*	*cuisinière*
tailor	*tailleur*	*tailleure*
cobbler	*cordonnier*	*cordonnière*
architect	*architecte*	*architecte*
engineer	*ingénieur*	*ingénieur*
baker	*boulanger*	*boulangère*
grocer	*épicier*	*épicière*
writer	*écrivain*	*écrivaine*

postman	*facteur*	*factrice*
police-man	*agent de police*	*agent de police*
painter	*peintre*	*peintre*
driver	*chauffeur*	*chauffeur*
politician	*politicien*	*politicienne*
manager	*directeur*	*directrice*
lawyer	*juriste*	*juriste*
journalist	*journaliste*	*journaliste*
judge	*juge*	*juge*
banker	*banquier*	*banquier*
clerk	*employé*	*employée*
salesperson	*vendeur*	*vendeuse*
announcer	*présentateur*	*présentatrice*
artist	*artiste*	*artiste*
contractor	*entrepreneur*	*entrepreneuse*
photographer	*photographe*	*photographe*
author	*auteur*	*auteure*
publisher	*éditeur*	*éditrice*
accountant	*comptable*	*comptable*
editor	*éditeur*	*éditrice*
producer	*réalisateur*	*réalisatrice*
farmer	*agriculteur*	*agricultrice*

magician	*magicien*	*magicienne*
weaver	*tisserand*	*tisserande*
jeweller	*bijoutier*	*bijoutière*
chemist	*chimiste*	*chimiste*
blacksmith	*forgeron*	*forgeron*
goldsmith	*orfèvre*	*orfèvre*
barber	*coiffeur*	*coiffeuse*
sweeper	*balayeur*	*balayeuse*
gardener	*jardinier*	*jardinière*
fisherman	*pêcheur*	*pêcheuse*
carpenter	*charpentier*	*charpentier*
watchman	*gardien*	*gardienne*
nurse	*infirmier*	*infirmière*
mason	*maçon*	*maçon*
plumber	*plombier*	*plombier*
navigator	*navigateur*	*navigatrice*
cartoonist	*caricaturiste*	*caricaturiste*
commentator	*commentateur*	*commentatrice*
electrician	*électricien*	*électricienne*
computer engineer	*informaticien*	*informaticienne*
player	*joueur*	*joueuse*

painist	pianiste	pianiste
researcher	chercheur	chercheuse
detective	détective	détective
sportsperson	sportif	sportive
surgeon	chirugien	chirugienne
dentist	dentiste	dentiste
businessperson	homme d'affaires	femme d'affaires
student	étudiant	étudiante

Dialogue

A : What is your profession ?
Quelle est votre profession ?

B : I am a doctor.
Je sius médecin.

A : What does your father do ?
Que fait votre père ?

B : My father is a dentist.
Mon père est dentiste.

A : What does your mother do ?
Que fait votre mère ?

B : My mother is a housewife.
Ma mère est femme au foyer.

Before a profession, the article is never used.

Ex. I am *an* author
Je suis auteur.

38

CLOTHES
LES VÊTEMENTS

MATERIAL
MATÉRIEL

cloth	*tissue*
wool	*laine*
silk	*soie*
cotton	*coton*
leather	*cuir*
polyester	*polyester*
nylon	*nylon*
chiffon	*mousseline*

To ask about the material, we use the expression

"*En quoi est . . . . . .*"

Ex : What is the shirt made of ?
En quoi est la chemise ?

To mention the material, we can use two prepositions "*de*" and "*en*".

Ex : The shirt is made of cotton.
La chemise est en coton.
La chemise est de coton.

The above two sentences can be literally translated as
The shirt is in cotton.
The shirt is of cotton.

VOCABULARY

outfit	*l'habit*
costume	*le costume*
dress	*la robe*
skirt	*la jupe*
blouse	*le blouson*
scarf	*l' écharpe*
trousers	*le pantalon*
shirt	*la chemise*
cap	*le chapeau*
tie	*la cravate*
stockings	*le bas*
belt	*la ceinture*
socks	*les chaussures*
bow	*le nœud-papillon*
coat	*le manteau*
waistcoat	*le gilet*
overcoat	*le pardessus*
raincoat	*l'imperméable*

jacket	*la veste*
sweater	*le pull-over*
suit	*le complet*
gown	*la robe*
t-shirt	*le t-shirt*
underwear	*les sous-vêtements*
gloves	*les gants*
sleeve	*la manche*
napkin	*la serviette*
hankerchief	*le mouchoir*
shorts	*les culottes*
sportswear	*les vêtements de sport*
muffler	*le cache-nez*
night suit	*les vêtements de nuit*
evening dress	*l'habit de soirée*

39

LODGING
LE LOGEMENT

Vocabulary

country	*un pays*
continent	*un continent*
city/town	*une ville*
suburb	*un banlieu*
village	*un village*
building	*un bâtiment*
house	*une maison*
flat	*un immeuble*
apartment	*un apartement*
studio flat	*un studio*
hut	*une hulte*
villa	*une villa*
room	*la pièce*
bedroom	*la chambre*
kitchen	*la cuisine*
dining room	*la salle à manger*
drawing room	*le salon*

bathroom	*la salle de bains*
toilet	*les toilettes*
entrance	*l'entrée*
corridor	*le couloir*
attic	*le grenier*
garage	*le garage*
basement	*la cave*
roof	*le toit*
wall	*le mur*
door	*la porte*
ground floor	*le rez-de-chaussée*
first floor	*le premier étage*
window	*la fenêtre*
floor	*le plafond*
ceiling	*le plancher*
staircase	*l'escalier*
big	*grand*
small	*petit*
ancient	*ancien*
modern	*moderne*
well-lit	*clair*
dull	*sombre*

isolated	*isolé*
calm	*calme*
noisy	*bruyant*
agreeable	*agréable*
comfortable	*confortable*
practical	*pratique*
to sell	*vendre*
on sale	*à vendre*
to buy	*acheter*
to rent	*louer*
landlord	*le propriétaire*
tenant	*le locataire*

40

JEWELLERY
BIJOUX

Vocabulary

Ring	*une bague*
Ear-ring	*une boucle d'oreille*
Bracelet	*un bracelet*
Pendant	*un pendentif*
Bangle	*un bracelet*
Necklace	*un collier*
Nose-ring	*un anneau de nez*
Armlet	*un brassard*
Anklet	*un anneau de cheville*
Chain	*une chaîne*
Gold	*l'or*
Silver	*l'argent*
Diamond	*le diamant*
Emerald	*l'émeraude*
Ruby	*le rubis*
Sapphire	*le saphir*
Zircon	*le zircon*
Turquoise	*la turquoise*

Real pearl	*la perle fine*
Cultured pearl	*la perle de culture*
Opal	*l'opale*
Cat's eye	*l'œil de chat*
Coral	*le corail*

Dialogue

A : I just bought a necklace.
Je viens d'acheter un collier.

B : Made of gold or silver ?
En or ou en argent ?

A : I bought a diamond necklace, with a bracelet in gold.
J'ai acheté un collier de diamants avec un bracelet en or.

B : My husband gave me a bracelet with emeralds and ruby.
Mon mari m'a donné un bracelet d'émeraudes et de rubis.

A : Do you have pearl earings ?
Avez-vous des boucles d'oreilles de perle ?

B : But I have cultured pearls, not real.
Mais j'ai les perles de culture, pas de perles fines.

A : You have a beautiful collection of jewellery.
Vous avez une belle collection de bijoux.

41

HOUSE-HOLD ARTICLES AND FURNITURE
APPAREIL MÉNAGERS ET MEUBLES

THE HOUSE-HOLD GOODS
LES APPAREILS MÉNAGERS

Cupboard	*un armoire*
Mirror	*un miroir*
Fan	*un ventilateur*
Airconditioner	*un climatiseur*
Heater	*un appareil de chauffage*
Central heating	*un chauffage central*
Clock	*une horloge*
Bedside table	*une table de nuit*
Dressing table	*une coiffeuse*
Bed	*un lit*
Blanket	*une couverture*
Bedsheet	*un drap de lit*
Bedcover	*un couvre-lit*
Pillow	*un oreiller*
Cushion	*un coussin*
Wash basin	*un lavabo*

Bathtub	*une baignoire*
Sink (in a kitchen)	*un évier*
Shower	*une douche*
Bucket	*un seau*
Soap	*un savon*
Shampoo	*un shampooing*
Toothpaste	*une pâte dentifrice*
Toothbrush	*une brosse à dents*
Razor	*un rasoir*
Electric razor	*un rasoir électrique*
Brush	*une brosse*
Comb	*un peigne*
Detergent	*un détersif*
Sink (in a bathroom)	*un lavabo*
Toilet-paper	*un papier hygiénique*
Toilet soap	*une savonnette*
Dinner plate	*une grande assiette*
Pressure cooker	*un auto-cuiseur*
Frying pan	*une poêle*
Tea-pot	*une bouilloire*
Tea set	*un service à thé*
Tea-tray	*un plateau à thé*
Serving spoon	*une grande cuiller*

Fork	*une fourchette*
Knife	*un couteau*
Spoon	*une cuiller*
Teaspoon	*une petite cuiller*
Tablespoon	*une cuiller de service*
Washing machine	*une machine à laver*
Dish washer	*un lave-vaisselle*
Broom-stick	*une manche à balai*
Iron	*un fer*
Refrigerator	*un réfrigérateur*
Microwave	*un four à micro-ondes*
Oven	*un four*
Lipstick	*le rouge*
Blusher	*le fard à joues*
Nailpolish	*le vernis*
Powder	*la poudre*
Eye-liner	*le eye-liner*
Mascara	*le mascara*
Face-pack	*un masque*
Carpet	*un tapis*
Untensils	*une vaisselle*
Eye-shadow	*le fard à paupières*

42

TREES
ARBRES

Vocabulary

A seed	*une graine*
A germ	*un embryon*
A bud	*un bourgeon*
A plant	*une plante*
A root	*une racine*
A stem	*une tige*
A branch	*une branche*
A trunk	*un tronc*
A leaf	*une feuille*
A fruit	*un fruit*
A flower	*une fleur*
A bark	*une écorce*
Fiber	*une fibre*
Bamboo	*un bambou*
Coconut	*un cocotier*
Wood	*un bois*
Gum	*un gommier*

Cactus	*un cactus*
Tamarind	*un tamarinier*
A pine tree	*un pin*
A banyan tree	*un banian*
A palm tree	*un palmier*
An apple tree	*un pommier*
A mango tree	*un manguier*
A walnut tree	*un noyer*
A cherry tree	*un cerisier*
Teak	*un tek*
Skin	*une peau*
An oak tree	*un chêne*
A lime tree	*un tilleul*
A mulberry tree	*un mûrier*
Sandal	*un santal*
Acacia	*un acacia*
A banana tree	*un bananier*
An orange tree	*un oranger*
A rubber tree	*un arbre à gomme*
An almond tree	*un amandier*
A tulip tree	*un tulipier*
A magnolia tree	*un magnolier*

43

FLOWERS
FLEURS

Vocabulary

A petal	*un pétale*
A pollen	*un pollen*
Allspice	*le quatre-épices*
Lily	*le lis*
Lotus	*le lotus*
Rose	*la rose*
Sunflower	*le tournesol*
Bluebell	*la jacinthe des bois*
Chrysanthemum	*le chrysanthème*
Orchid	*l'orchidée*
Dahlia	*le dahlia*
Jasmine	*le jasmin*
Marigold	*le souci*
Crab apple	*la pomme sauvage*
Camellia	*le camélia*
Azalea	*l'azalée*
Daffodil	*la jonquille*

Magnolia	le magnolia
Diana	la diane
Violet	la violette
Peony	la pivoine
Peach blossom	la fleur de pêcher
Orchis	l'orchis
Water lily	le nénuphar
Daisy	la pâquerette
Coltsfoot	le tussilage
Celandine	la chélidoine
Chervil	le cerfeuil
Cowslip	la primevère
Campion	le lychnis
Dandelion	le pissenlit
Forget-me-not	le myosotis
Groundsel	le séneçon
Kingcup	le souci d'eau
Buttercup	le bouton d'or
Lily of the valley	le muguet
Primrose	la primevère
Shephard's purse	la bourse à pasteur
Snowdrop	la perce-neige
Wood aremone	l'anémone des bois

44

ANIMALS
ANIMAUX

Vocabulary

an animal	*un animal*
a bird	*un oiseau*
an insect	*un insecte*
an amphibian	*un amphibie*
a reptile	*un reptile*
a mammal	*un mamifère*
herbivorous	*herbivore*
carnivorous	*carnivore*
omnivorous	*omnivore*
an egg	*un oeuf*
a beak	*un bec*
a paw	*une patte*
a tail	*une queue*
a coat	*un pelage*
a skin	*une peau*
a scale	*une écaille*
a fin	*une nageoire*

gills	*des branchies*
a horn	*une corne*
a trunk	*une trompe*
a hump	*une bosse*
a feather	*une plume*
a claw	*une griffe*
a wing	*un aile*
a nest	*un nid*
a domestic animal	*un animal domestique*
a wild animal	*un animal sauvage*
a swarm	*un essaim*
a bee-hive	*une ruche*
a spider-web	*une toile*
a swallow	*une hirondelle*
a dogbite	*une morsure de chien*
a snakebite	*une morsure de serpent*
a dog	*un chien*
a mouse	*une souris*
a hamster	*un hamster*
a rabbit	*un lapin*
a cat	*un chat*
a guinea pig	*un cochon d'Inde*

a horse	*un cheval*
a parrot	*un perroquet*
a budgerigar	*une perruche*
a fish	*un poisson*
a gold fish	*un poisson rouge*
a tarantula	*une tarentule*
a tortoise	*une tortue*
a chicken	*une poule*
a cock	*un coq*
a lion	*un lion*
a tiger	*un tigre*
an elephant	*un éléphant*
a crocodile	*un crocodile*
a rhinoceros	*un rhinocéros*
a monkey	*un singe*
a gazelle	*une gazelle*
a bear	*un ours*
a snake	*un serpent*
a rat	*un rat*
a mosquito	*un moustique*
a fly	*une mouche*
an ox	*un bœuf*

an ant	*une fourmi*
a cicada	*une cigale*
a caterpillar	*une chenille*
a butterfly	*un papillon*
a dragonfly	*une libellule*
a grasshopper	*une sauterelle*
a cricket	*un grillon*
a spider	*une araignée*
a flea	*une puce*
a louse	*un pou*
a bee	*une abeille*
a wasp	*une guêpe*
a sparrow	*un moineau*
a lark	*une allouette*
a crow	*un corbeau*
a canary	*un canari*
an eagle	*un aigle*
a magpie	*une pie*
an owl	*un hibou*
an ostrich	*une autruche*
a gull	*une mouette*
a penguin	*un pingouin*

a worm	*un ver*
a viper	*une vipère*
a grass snake	*une couleuvre à collier*
a rattlesnake	*un serpent à sonnettes*
a lizard	*un lézard*
a crocodile	*un crocodile*
a frog	*une grenouille*
a toad	*un crapaud*
a duck	*un canard*
a cobra	*un serpent à lunettes*
a secretary bird	*un serpentaire*
an alligator	*un alligator*
a buffalo	*un buffle*
a camel	*un chameau*
a centipede	*un mille-pattes*
a crane	*une grue*
a cow	*une vache*
a deer	*un cerf*
a dolphin	*un dauphin*
a dragon	*un dragon*
an earthworm	*un ver de terre*
a fox	*un renard*

a giraffe	*une girafe*
a gorilla	*un gorille*
a hippopotamus	*un hippopotame*
a jackal	*un chacal*
a kangaroo	*un kangourou*
a lion	*un lion*
a leopard	*un léopard*
a mongoose	*une mangouste*
a mule	*un mulet*
a panda	*un panda*
a pig	*un cochon*
a scorpion	*un scorpion*
a sea lion	*une otarie*
a seal	*un phoque*
a shark	*un requin*
a sheep	*un mouton*
a snail	*un escargot*
a squirrel	*un écureuil*
a swan	*un cygne*
a zebra	*un zèbre*
a cuckoo	*un coucou*
a dove	*une colombe*

a drone	*un faux-bourdon*
a goose	*une oie*
a peacock	*un paon*
a wood-pecker	*un pic*
a pigeon	*un pigeon*
an octopus	*une pieuvre*
an oyster	*une huître*
a sea horse	*un hippocampe*
a seagull	*une mouette*

45

MEDIA
LES MÉDIAS

Vocabulary

PRESS
LA PRESSE

a newspaper	*un journal*
a daily	*un quotidien*
a weekly	*un hebdomadaire*
a bi-monthly	*un bi-mensuel*
a half-yearly	*un semestriel*
a yearly	*un annuel*
a magazine	*un magazine*
an article	*un article*
a heading	*un titre*
a headline	*un gros titre*
a subject	*un sujet*
an advertisement	*une annonce*
a classified	*une petite annonce*
an issue	*un numéro*
a subscription	*un abonnement*

RADIO
LA RADIO

a programme	*une émission*
a commercial radio station	*une station commerciale*
a programme	*un programme*
a radio set	*une poste de radio*

TELEVISION
LA TÉLÉVISION

a television set	*un téléviseur*
a colour T.V.	*une télé en couleurs*
a black & white T.V.	*une télé en noir et blanc*
a screen	*un écran*
a button	*un bouton*
a remote	*une télécommande*

46

FAMILY
LA FAMILLE

Vocabulary

family member	*le membre de la famille*
parents	*les parents*
mother	*la mère*
father	*le père*
brother	*le frère*
sister	*la sœur*
grandparents	*les grand parents*
grandfather	*le grand-père*
grandmother	*la grand mère*
son	*le fils*
daughter	*la fille*
grandson	*le petit-fils*
grand daughter	*la petite-fille*
grandchild	*le petit-enfant*
husband	*le mari*
wife	*la femme*
spouse	*l'épouse*

fiancé	*le fiancé*
father-in-law	*le beau-père*
mother-in-law	*la belle-mère*
son-in-law	*le gendre*
daughter-in-law	*la belle-fille*
brother-in-law	*le beau-frère*
sister-in-law	*la belle-soeur*
aunt	*la tante*
uncle	*l'oncle*
neighbour	*le voisin*
cousin brother	*le cousin*
cousin sister	*la cousine*
nephew	*le neveu*
niece	*la nièce*
elder brother	*le frère aîné.*
younger brother	*le frère cadet*
elder sister	*la sœur aînée*
younger sister	*la sœur cadette*
child	*l'enfant*
offspring	*la progéniture*

47

THE AUTOMOBILE
AUTOMOBILE

Vocabulary

The car	*la voiture*
The car	*l'auto*
The body	*la carrosserie*
The wing	*l'aile*
The roof	*le toit*
The bumper	*le pare-chocs*
The wheel	*la roue*
The tyre	*le pneu*
The spare wheel	*la roue de secours*
The engine	*le moteur*
The bonnet	*le capot*
The door	*la portière*
The window	*la vitre*
The windscreen	*le pare-brise*
The viper	*l'essuie-glace*
The seat	*le siège*
The steering wheel	*le volant*

The rear-view mirror	le rétroviseur
The lighting	l'éclairage
The head light	le phare
The number plate	la plaque d'immatriculation
The brake	le break
The gear box	la boîte de vitesse
The pedal	la pédale
The silencer	le silencieux
The clutch plate	le disque d'embrayage
The accelerator	l'accélérateur
The indicator	l'indicateur
The indicator light	le clignotant
The horn	le klaxon
The driving	la conduite
The driver	le chauffeur
To drive	conduire
To break	démarrer
To accelerate	accélérer
To move forward	avancer
To run	rouler
To reverse	reculer
To turn left	tourner à gauche

To turn right	*tourner à droite*
To take a U-turn	*faire demi-tour*
To cross	*croiser*
To overtake	*dépasser*
	doubler une autre voiture
To break	*freiner*
To stop	*s'arrêter*
To park	*se garer*
	stationner
To be out of order	*être en panne*
To repair	*réparer*
The repairing	*la réparation*
To fix	*dépanner*
The fixing	*le dépannage*
The garage	*le garage*
The garagist	*le garagiste*
The service-station	*la station service*
The petrol pump	*le poste d'essence*
Petrol	*l'essence*
The pumpist	*le pompiste*
The tank	*le réservoir*
Full	*plein*

Empty	*vide*
Flat tyre	*la roue est à plat*
To inflate	*gonfler*
Oil level	*le niveau de l'huile*
Tyre pressure	*la pression des pneus*
To exceed the speed limit	*faire un excès de vitesse*
To give a fine	*avoir une amend*
A fine	*une contravention*
To cross a red light	*brûler un feu rouge*
To hit a tree	*heurter un arbre*
To enter into	*rentrer dans*
To avoid an accident	*éviter un accident*
To crush an animal	*écraser un chien*
To break	*abîmer* *casser*
To damage	*endommager*
To knock over	*renverser*

48

TRANSPORT
TRANSPORTS

Vocabulary

Modes of transport	*les moyens de transport*
A vehicle	*une véhicule*
An automobile	*un automobile*
A car	*une voiture*
	une auto
A bus	*un autobus*
A train	*un train*
A plane	*un avion*
A motorbike	*une moto*
A cycle	*une vélo*
A metro	*un métro*
A boat	*un bateau*
A liner	*un paquebot*
A ship	*une navire*
A shuttle	*une navette*
A rocket	*une fusée*
A truck	*un camion*

A bulldozer	*un bulldozer*
A hovercraft	*un aéroglisseur*
A taxi	*un taxi*
A bicycle	*une bicyclette*
A horsecar	*un fourgon à chevaux*
A tram	*un tram*
A trolley bus	*un trolleybus*
A three-wheeler	*une voiture à trois roues*
A tricycle	*un tricycle*
A tractor	*un tracteur*
A trainer-aircraft	*un avion-école*
A jeep	*une jeep*
A van	*un fourgon*
A fire-engine	*une voiture de pompiers*
An ambulance	*une ambulance*
A rickshaw (pulled by a man)	*un pousse-pousse*
A rickshaw (pulled by bicycle)	*un rickshaw*
A crane	*une grue*
A motorboat	*un bateau à moteur*
A tanker	*un camion-citerne*
A rowing boat	*un canot*

A yacht	*un yacht*
A sailboat	*un voilier*
A lifeboat	*un canot de sauvetage*
A cargo boat	*un cargo*
A cargo plane	*un avion-cargo*
A glider	*un planeur*
A helicopter	*un hélicoptère*
A jet	*un jet*
A jet fighter	*un chasseur à réaction*
A moped	*un vélomoteur*
On foot	*a pied*

To talk about a mode of transport, we can use any of the following ways :

1. The verb "*utiliser*" (to use). For example,

   I use the tram for going to the market.
   J'utilise le tram pour aller au marché.

2. The verb "*prendre*" (to take). For example,

   I take the bus for going to school.
   Je prends le bus pour aller à l'école.

3. The expression "*par le/la/l'/les*" (by the). For example,

   I go to school by the metro.
   Je vais à l'école par le métro.

I go to Paris by the plane.
*Je vais à Paris **par** l'avion.*

I go to the cinema by the car.
*Je vais au cinéma **par la** voiture.*

4. The preposition *"en"* (in). For example,

We go from Delhi to Agra in a train.
*Nous allons de Delhi à Agra **en** train.*

He moves around in a car.
*Il circule **en** voiture.*

But there are exceptions with *moto* (motorbike), *vélo* (cycle), *bycyclette* (bicycle), *pied* (foot), *vélomoteur* (moped). We use the preposition *"à"* instead of *en*. For example,

Diego goes to the university on a bike.
*Diego va à l'université **à** moto.*

She goes to the market on foot.
*Elle va au marché **à** pied.*

49

COMPUTER
ORDINATEUR

Vocabulary

monitor	*le moniteur*
CPU	*UC*
URL	*URL*
scanner	*le scanneur*
printer	*l'imprimante*
keyboard	*le clavier*
hardware	*le hardware*
software	*le logiciel*
modem	*le modem*
CD-ROM	*le CD-ROM*
floppy disk	*la disquette*
memory	*la mémoire*
windows	*la fenêtre*
backup memory	*la mémoire auxiliare*
Internet	*l'internet*
graphics	*le traitement graphique*
multimedia	*la multimédia*

information technology	l'informatique
hard disk	le disque dur
processor	le processeur
processing unit	l'unité de traitement
RAM	RAM
database	la base de données
mouse	la souris
drive	l'unité de disques
speaker	l'enceite
DOS	DOS
microphone	le microphone
laser printer	l'imprimante laser
To install	installer
To download	télécharger
mouse pad	le tapis pour souris
downloading	le téléchargement
installation	l'installation
laser disk	le disque laser
microcomputer	le micro-ordinateur
data	les données
database manager	le logiciel de gestion de base de données
RAM chip	le barette mémoire

sound card	*la carte son*
hard copy	*le tirage*
hard disk drive	*l'unité de disque dur*
hard-wired	*câblé*
graphic display	*la visualisation graphique*
graphical display unit	*le visuel graphique*
graphical user interface	*l'interface graphique*
Internet café	*le cybercafé*
e-mail	*le courrier électronique*
memory capacity	*la capacité mémoire*
memory card	*la carte d'extension mémoire*
memory chip	*la puce mémoire*
floppy drive	*le lecteur de disquettes*
CD-ROM drive	*le lecteur de CD-ROM*
software engineer	*l' ingénieur logiciel*
software package	*le progiciel*
software engineering	*le génie logiciel*